TINSELTOWNS

STARRING

TOWNS AND CITIES FEATURED IN MOVIES AND TV SHOWS

A CAST OF THOUSANDS!

by John Kremer

Published by:

Ad-Lib Publications
51 N. Fifth Street
P. O. Box 1102
Fairfield, IA 52556-1102
(515) 472-6617

Printed in the United States of America

Library of Congress Cataloging in Publication Data
Kremer, John, 1949-
Tinseltowns, U.S.A.: starring towns and cities featured in movies
    and TV shows, a cast of thousands!

    p. 144   cm.
    Includes indexes.
    1. Cities and towns in motion pictures – United States –
Miscellanea. 2. Cities and towns in television – United States –
Miscellanea.   I. Title
PN1995.9.C513K74   1988   791.43'09'093217 – dc19   88-22186
ISBN 0-912411-21-X : $13.95.   ISBN 0-912411-18-X (pbk.) : $6.95

Table of Contents

Introduction – A Note from the Author

The producers of the **Mary Tyler Moore Show** can claim some responsibility for this book, because her show was one of the first hit TV series to make active and substantial use of its regional locale—in this case, Minneapolis, Minnesota. Since I was living in Minneapolis at the time, I was able to appreciate the added dimension of the show's regional situations and humor even more so than most viewers.

The success of the **Mary Tyler Moore Show**, of course, inspired the creators of other TV series to set their shows in various cities around the country (shows such as **Alice, WKRP, Happy Days, Mork and Mindy, Family Ties, One Day at a Time, Cheers, The Popcorn Kid, Mr. Belvedere, Amen,** and **Frank's Place**).

While the proliferation of TV shows with regional settings inspired this particular book, the idea of featuring towns and cities in a book first grew out of my interest in unusual town names (which, in turn, grew out of my interest in unusual words). By now I have a collection of several thousand odd, funny, intriguing, and/or wonderful town names.

On the following pages, I've listed a few of my favorite out-of-the-ordinary town names—names so much more interesting than the name of the town in which I now live (Fairfield, Iowa). Fairfield is about as commonplace a town name as you can get — there are 23 Fairfield's in the U.S.A. alone!

Here are a few of my favorite town names. I think you'll like them, too.

Holidays: Santa Claus, Indiana; North Pole, (Alaska, New York, and Colorado); Christmas (Arizona, Florida, and Michigan); Valentine (Arizona, Nebraska, and Texas) or Valentines, Virginia.

Characteristics: How would you like to live in Boring? If so, you have your choice: You can live in either Maryland, Missouri, or Oregon. You can also go to Missouri (as well as Virginia) if you want to be Bland. Want to be Carefree? Go to Arizona. Humble? Go to Texas. Looking for the Magic? Again, go to Texas.

Things: Looking for Cash? See Arkansas. Looking to find a Bonanza? Try Nevada, Oregon, or Texas. Need an Index. Go to Washington. Want to go Home? Go to Kansas or Pennsylvania. Want to put your nose to the Grindstone? Again, go to Pennyslvania.

Acronyms: Some town names are acronyms (where the word is made up of the beginning letters of other words—just as *radar* derives from the first letters of the following words: RAdio Detecting And Ranging, and *snafu* derives from Situation Normal, All Fouled Up). Here are a few acronymic town names: Alma, Georgia (made up of the initials of past and present capitals of Georgia: Augusta, Louisville, Milledgeville, and Atlanta); Alcoa, Tennessee (named for Alcoa, the ALuminum Company Of America); Jal, New Mexico (John A. Lynch, an east Texas rancher who sold cattle to the original town founders), and LeMars, Iowa (taken from the initial letters of the surnames of six young women who were present during an inspection visit of the town site).

Backwords: Lebam, Washington (derived from the backward spelling of Mabel, the daughter of the man who named the town).

Blends: Some town names are made up of blends. Blends are words consisting of a mix of two or more words. For example, *motel* is a blend of motor and hotel; *smog* is a blend of smoke and fog; and *brunch* is a blend of breakfast and lunch. Here are a few town names made up of blends: Adel, Iowa (a + dell); Calexico, California (California + Mexico); Orland, California (orange + land); Texarkana, Arkansas, and Texarkana, Texas (Texas + Arkansas + Louisiana); and Texico, New Mexico (Texas + New Mexico).

Reduplicatives: Some town names duplicate part or all of their name: Show Low, Arizona; Ty Ty, Georgia; and Walla Walla, Washington (one of my favorite town names).

Just for Fun: Did you know that there is both a Paradise and a Hell in Michigan? That you can find both Coldwater and Hot Coffee in Mississippi? That you can get caught in a Cyclone, a Hurricane, a Tornado, and a Whirlwind in West Virginia? That you can get a bite to eat in Sandwich, Illinois; or Sandwich, Massachusetts; or Sandwich, Nebraska? Or that it is possible to end up in either Matrimony or Old Trap (or both) in North Carolina?

These are just a few of the odd, or funny, or whimsical town names I've run across while doing the research for this book and the ones to follow. Even if you are not intrigued by these unusual town names but you are a movie fan or a couch potato, then you should still enjoy this book. Besides featuring over 400 towns and cities in the United States and Canada, this book also features more than 400 movies and 400 television shows. While some of the movies are quite old and, in some cases, deservedly forgotten and while some of the television shows had very short lives, most of the movies and television shows featured in this book are quite well known. I hope this book helps you to relive some of the best moments of those movies and TV shows.

To make this book more challenging, I've designed most of the bits and pieces of trivia as a series of quizzes. After you've tested your own memory on these quizzes, try them out on your friends. Note that at the top of the matching quizzes, I've indicated what would be a good score if you were a serious movie or TV fanatic [in other words, an expert]. To make it easier for you to find the correct answer to the various questions, the answers are printed in small type at the bottom of each page (if there is one thing I hate, it is having to flip back and forth in a quiz book to find the correct answers).

So, that's it. I hope you enjoy the book—and tell your friends about it.

Meanwhile, if you'd like to help me out with the other books in this series, turn to the last page of this book. It tells you how to write to me with suggestions, criticisms, comments, and marriage proposals. I'm open to all four, but they've got to be good. Thanks.

John Kremer
July 4, 1988

Towns and Cities
in the
Movies

Here's Your Ticket to the Movies

The first section of this book features over 400 movies in which various towns and cities have starred (or at least had a bit part). The movies themselves are a varied collection, from recent mega-hits to long forgotten oldies, from romantic comedies to action thrillers. Nonetheless, if you watch late-night movies or have a VCR, you've undoubtedly seen many of them.

I hope the following pages bring back many fond memories for you. If nothing else, they certainly will test your memory.

If you know of other movies where a town or city is featured prominently as part of the movie, please send me the information. I'll include any new contributions in future editions of this book. If you send me something I don't already have, I'll send you an autographed copy of the latest edition and will also list your name in the preface to the book. Send information to me at the following address: **John Kremer, c/o Ad-Lib Publications, 51 N. Fifth Street, Fairfield, IA 52556-3226.**

Thanks for your help.

Now it's your turn to enjoy. Read on!

Movie Firsts

There is a first time for everything. Here are a few movie firsts. How many do you know?

1. Where was the first live theater in the United States (1716)?

2. Who built the first movie studio, and where was it built?

3. Where and when was the first drive-in movie theater put into operation?

4. Where is the largest drive-in movie theater located?

5. What television station was the first to show films as part of its regular programming (1931)?

6. Where was the first motion picture production center of the world (from 1907 to 1916)?

1. Williamsburg, Virginia   2. Thomas Edison built the first movie studio, called the Black Maria, in West Orange, New Jersey, in 1892.   3. Camden, New Jersey, on June 6, 1933   4. Loew's Open Air Theater in Lynn, Massachusetts, holds 5000 automobiles.   5. W2XCD in Passaic, New Jersey   6. Fort Lee, New Jersey

Movie Musicals

1. The musical, **State Fair,** was made into a movie twice: once in 1945 (starring Jeanne Crain, Dana Andrews, and Dick Haymes) and a second time in 1962 (starring Pat Boone, Ann-Margaret, and Bobby Darin). The state fairs of these two movies were held in two different cities (and states). What were those cities?

2. Five years before he starred in **State Fair,** Pat Boone starred in the musical romance, **April Love** (with Shirley Jones). Where was this musical set?

3. John Travolta starred in two contemporary musical romances, **Saturday Night Fever** (1977) and **Urban Cowboy** (1980). In what two cities were these two movies set?

4. Honolulu, Hawaii, has been a favorite setting for musical romances. Can you name two musicals set in Honolulu?

5. Because of its musical heritage, New Orleans, Louisiana, is also a popular setting for musicals. Again, name two musicals set in New Orleans.

6. **The T.A.M.I. Show**, one of the first rockumentaries (1964), featured the Rolling Stones, Chuck Berry, James Brown, the Supremes, and many other top rock stars of that era. T.A.M.I., which stands for Teenage Awards Music International, was filmed in what civic auditorium?

7. The most famous of all rockumentaries (starring Joan Baez, Richie Havens, Crosby Stills & Nash, Jefferson Airplane, Joe Cocker, Country Joe and the Fish, Santana, Sha-Na-Na, Jimi Hendrix, The Who, and many others) was filmed in August of 1970 on a farm near what New York town?

8. The 1961 musical, **Flower Drum Song**, (starring Nancy Kwan, James Shigeta, and Miyoshi Umeki) featured the Chinatown of what large city?

9. **West Side Story**, the 1961 musical (starring Natalie Wood, Richard Beyner, Rita Moreno, and George Chakiris), is an updated version of *Romeo and Juliet* set in the streets of what city?

10. The following three movies featured biographies of various composers or musicians. Where were the movies set?

    a. **With a Song in My Heart**, 1952 biography of singer Jane Froman (starring Susan Hayward).

    b. **I Wonder Who's Kissing Her Now**, 1947 biography of vaudeville songwriter Joe Howard (starring June Haver and Mark Stevens).

    c. **Purple Rain**, the 1985 semi-autobiographical musical starring Prince.

11. Perhaps the most famous musical of them all is **Singin' in the Rain**, starring Gene Kelly, Debbie Reynolds, Donald O'Connor, Jean Hagen, and Cyd Charisse. Where was it set?

12. **Centennial Summer** was a 1946 musical (starring Jeanne Crain, Cornel Wilde, and Linda Darnell) set at the 1876 centennial celebration of the founding of the country. Where was it set?

13. **The Unsinkable Molly Brown** (starring Debbie Reynolds) was from what city?

---

1. 1945: Des Moines, Iowa; 1962: Dallas, Texas 2. Lexington, Kentucky 3. New York (Brooklyn), New York; Houston, Texas (Pasadena, Texas) 4. Blue Hawaii (with Elvis Presley); The Revolt of Mamie Stover (with Jane Russell); and Waikiki Wedding (with Bing Crosby) 5. Birth of the Blues (Bing Crosby), King Creole (with Elvis Presley), Mardi Gras (with Pat Boone) 6. Santa Monica, California 7. Woodstock, New York 8. San Francisco, California 9. New York, New York 10. a. Saint Louis, Missouri b. Weehawken, New Jersey c. Minneapolis, Minnesota 11. Hollywood, California 12. Philadelphia, Pennsylvania 13. Denver, Colorado

Broadcast News: Holly Hunter, William Hurt, Albert Brooks © 20th Century Fox / Shooting Star

Romance at the Movies

1. College life is almost always conducive to romances. Can you name the location of the following college romances?

   a. **Hold 'Em, Yale**, 1935 starring Buster Crabbe and Cesar Romero

   b. **She Loves Me Not**, 1934 starring Bing Crosby and Miriam Hopkins

   c. **Love Story**, 1970 starring Ryan O'Neal and Ali MacGraw

   d. **Where the Boys Are**, 1960 starring George Hamilton and Yvette Mimieux

   e. **Winter Carnival**, 1939 starring Richard Carlson and Ann Sheridan

2. **High Society** (starring Bing Crosby, Grace Kelly and Frank Sinatra) was a 1956 remake of an earlier romantic classic, **The _____ Story** (starring James Stewart, Cary Grant, and Katherine Hepburn). Where were both of these movies set?

3. Roger Vadim's 1988 remake of his classic, **And God Created Woman**, starred Rebecca DeMornay (the original starred Brigitte Bardot). The original was filmed in St. Tropez, France. What city was used as the location for the remake?

4. William Hurt, Holly Hunter, and Albert Brooks were involved in a romantic triangle in the 1987 movie, **Broadcast News**. In what city was their TV station located?

1. a. New Haven, Connecticut   b. Princeton, New Jersey   c. Cambridge, Massachusetts   d. Fort Lauderdale, Florida   e. Hanover, New Hampshire
2. Philadelphia, Pennsylvania   3. Santa Fe, New Mexico   4. Washington, D.C.

More Romantic Movies

Where were the following movie romances set? [Expert rating: 9 out of 13]

1. **Barefoot in the Park,** 1967 starring Jane Fonda and Robert Redford
2. **The Barefoot Mailman,** 1951 starring Bob Cummings and Terry Moore
3. **Beneath the 12 Mile Reef,** 1953 starring Robert Wagner and Terry Moore
4. **Chicken Every Sunday,** 1949 starring Dan Dailey and Celeste Holm
5. **Cinderella Liberty,** 1973 starring James Caan and Marsha Mason
6. **Duchess of Idaho,** 1950 starring Esther Williams
7. **Flashdance,** 1983 starring Jennifer Beals and Michael Nouri
8. **The Front Page,** 1930 starring Adolphe Menjou, Pat O'Brien, Mary Brian
9. **The Girls on the Beach,** 1965 starring Linda Marshall and Noreen Corcoran
10. **Glory Alley,** 1952 starring Ralph Meeker and Leslie Caron
11. **Hot Dog: The Movie,** 1984 starring David Naughton and Patrick Houser
12. **I Could Never Have Sex,** 1973 romance starring Gail and Martin Stayden
13. **I Will ... I Will ... For Now,** 1976 starring Diane Keaton and Elliot Gould

a. Chicago, Illinois
b. Key West, Florida
c. Martha's Vineyard, Massachusetts
d. Miami, Florida
e. New Orleans, Louisiana
f. New York, New York
g. Pittsburgh, Pennsylvania
h. Santa Barbara, California
i. Santa Monica, California
j. Seattle, Washington
k. Squaw Valley, California
l. Sun Valley, Idaho
m. Tucson, Arizona

Answers: 1. f   2. d   3. b   4. m   5. j   6. l   7. g   8. a   9. i   10. e   11. k   12. c   13. h

Even More Romantic Movies

Here are some more movie romances to match with their location. [Expert rating: 8 out of 12]

1. **Ice Castles**, 1979 starring Lynn-Holly Johnson and Robby Benson
2. **Meet the Girls**, 1938 starring June Lang, Lynn Bari, and Robert Allen
3. **Mischief**, 1985 starring Doug McKeon, Kelly Preston, Chris Nash
4. **Miss Susie Slagle's**, 1945 starring Lillian Gish and Veronica Lake
5. **Nadine**, 1987 starring Jeff Bridges and Kim Basinger
6. **The Only Game in Town**, 1970 starring Elizabeth Taylor and Warren Beatty
7. **Short Circuit**, 1986 starring Ally Sheedy and Steve Guttenberg
8. **The Sweet Ride**, 1968 starring Tony Franciosa and Jacqueline Bisset
9. **The More, The Merrier**, 1946 starring Jean Arthur and Joel McCrea
10. **Three Little Girls in Blue**, 1946 starring June Haver, George Montgomery
11. **Top Gun**, 1986 starring Tom Cruise and Kelly McGillis
12. **Violets Are Blue**, 198? starring Sissy Spacek and Keven Kline

a. Astoria, Oregon
b. Atlantic City, New Jersey
c. Austin, Texas
d. Baltimore, Maryland
e. Honolulu, Hawaii
f. Las Vegas, Nevada
g. Malibu, California
h. Miramar, California
i. Nelsonville, Ohio
j. Ocean City, Maryland
k. Saint Paul, Minnesota
l. Washington, D.C.

Answers: 1. k   2. e   3. i   4. d   5. c   6. f   7. a   8. g   9. l   10. b   11. h   12. j

Movies of the 1920's and 1930's

Can you match the following dramatic movies with their locations? [Expert rating: 8 out of 10]

1. **Boys Town**, 1938 starring Spencer Tracy and Mickey Rooney
2. **The Buccaneer**, 1938 starring Frederic March (also 1958, Yul Bryner)
3. **Gone with the Wind**, 1939 starring Clark Gable and Vivian Leigh
4. **Greed**, 1925 classic starring Gibson Gowland, ZaSu Pitts, Jean Hersholt
5. **King of Gamblers**, 1937 starring Lloyd Nolan and Claire Trevor
6. **Little Women**, 1919 starring Lillian Hall, Isabel Lamon (also 1933, 1948)
7. **Road Demon**, 1938 starring Henry Arthur and Thomas Beck
8. **The Scarlet Letter**, 1926 starring Lillian Gish and Lars Hanson
9. **Tail Spin**, 1939 starring Alice Faye, Nancy Kelly, and Joan Davis
10. **Young Mr. Lincoln**, 1939 starring Henry Fonda and Alice Brady

a. Atlanta, Georgia
b. Cleveland, Ohio
c. Concord, Massachusetts
d. Indianapolis, Indiana
e. Las Vegas, Nevada
f. New Orleans, Louisiana
g. Omaha, Nebraska
h. Salem, Massachusetts
i. San Francisco, California
j. Springfield, Illinois

Answers: 1. g (and Boys Town, Nebraska)   2. f   3. a (as well as Jonesboro, Georgia)   4. i   5. e   6. c   7. d   8. h   9. b   10. j

Dramatic Movies of the 1940's

Match the following dramatic movies of the 1940's with their locations. Note that two movies were located in Boston and two in San Francisco. [Expert rating: 6 out of 10]

1. **Beyond Glory**, 1948 starring Alan Ladd and Audie Murphy
2. **Crash Drive**, 1943 starring Tyrone Power, Anne Baxter, Dana Andrews
3. **The Fighting Sullivans**, 1944 starring Anne Baxter and Thomas Mitchell
4. **The Foxes of Harrow**, 1947 starring Rex Harrison and Maureen O'Hara
5. **The Great Moment**, 1944 starring Joel McCrea, Harry Carey, Betty Field
6. **I Remember Mama**, 1948 starring Irene Dunne and Ellen Corby
7. **King's Row**, 1941 starring Ronald Reagan, Bob Cummings, Ann Sheridan
8. **Nob Hill**, 1945 starring George Raft and Joan Bennett
9. **Reaching for the Sun**, 1941 starring Joel McCrea and Ellen Drew
10. **The Shocking Miss Pilgrim**, 1947 starring Betty Grable
11. **To the Shores of Tripoli**, 1942 starring John Payne

a. Boston, Massachusetts
b. Boston, Massachusetts
c. Detroit, Michigan
d. Fulton, Missouri
e. New London, Connecticut
f. New Orleans, Louisiana
g. San Diego, California
h. San Francisco, California
i. San Francisco, California
j. Waterloo, Iowa
k. West Point, New York

Answers: 1. k   2. e   3. j   4. f   5. a / b   6. h / i   7. d   8. h / i   9. c   10. a / b   11. g

White Christmas: Danny Kaye and Bing Crosby   © Paramount Pictures / Shooting Star

Fictional Towns in Movies

1. In what fictional village did the 1954 musical **White Christmas** (starring Bing Crosby, Danny Kaye, Rosemary Clooney, and Vera-Ellen) take place?

2. **Red Dawn** (1984 drama starring Patrick Swayze) describes a Soviet invasion of the United States. In what fictional town did the high school students fight back?

3. **True Stories**, starring David Byrne, took place in what fictional town?

4. The 1948 drama, **The Walls of Jericho** (starring Cornel Wilde and Linda Darnell), tells the story of an ambitious lawyer in the small town of Jericho. In what state was Jericho located?

5. The 1956 western, **The Proud Ones** (starring Robert Ryan, Virginia Mayo, Jeffrey Hunter, and Walter Brennan) takes place in what fictional town?

6. Paul Newman and Joanne Woodward starred in the 1958 drama, **Rally 'Round the Flag, Boys!**, about a small town opposing the building of a missile base. What was the name of this town?

7. What town was the model for Gopher Prairie, the small town satirized in Sinclair Lewis's 1920 novel, **Main Street**?

8. What town served as the model for Sherwood Anderson's famous novel, **Winesburg, Ohio**?

1. Pine Tree, Vermont 2. Calumet, Colorado 3. Virgil, Texas 4. Kansas 5. Flat Rock, Kansas 6. Putnam's Landing, New York
7. Sauk Centre, Minnesota 8. Clyde, Ohio (Anderson's home town)

Dramatic Movies of the 1950's

1. Can you name the location for the following three 1950's dramas?

   a. **Compulsion**, 1959 starring Orson Welles and Diane Varsi

   b. **Little Egypt**, 1951 starring Mark Stevens and Rhonda Fleming

   c. **Party Girl**, 1958 starring Cyd Charisse and Robert Taylor

2. Can you name the setting for the following two dramas?

   a. **Panic in the Streets**, 1950 starring Richard Widmark and Paul Douglas

   b. **A Streetcar Named Desire**, 1951 starring Marlon Brando, Vivian Leigh, and Kim Hunter

3. The 1953 war drama, **From Here to Eternity**, starred Burt Lancaster, Deborah Kerr, Montgomery Clift, Frank Sinatra, Donna Reed, and Ernest Borgnine. Where was this movie set? Hint: The movie is famous for its love scene on the beach.

4. The following two 1950's movies were set on military bases. Can you name the bases?

   a. **Take the High Ground**, 1953 starring Richard Widmark and Karl Malden

   b. **Thundering Jets**, 1958 starring Rex Reason, Dick Foran, Audrey Dalton

5. The 1954 prison drama, **Riot in Cell Block 11**, starred Neville Brand. Where is Cell Block 11 located?

6. Two 1950's dramas were set in Arizona. Can you name the towns that were used as the settings for the following two movies?

a. **Arena**, 1953 rodeo drama starring Gig Young, Jean Hagen, and Polly Bergen

b. **Violent Saturday**, 1955 holdup drama starring Victor Mature, Richard Egan, and Lee Marvin

7. The 1957 movie, **The Abductors**, starred Victor McLaglen as a man attempting to rob Lincoln's grave. Where is Lincoln's grave?

8. **A Man Called Peter** was a 1955 biographical movie starring Richard Todd as Peter Marshall, a famous clergyman. Where did Peter Marshall have his congregation?

9. Montgomery Clift starred in the 1953 Alfred Hitchcock mystery drama, **I Confess**, about a priest who hears a killer's confession (and who is later accused of the crime himself). Where was this movie set?

1. All three were set in Chicago, Illinois. 2. New Orleans, Louisiana 3. Honolulu, Hawaii 4. a. Fort Bliss, Texas b. Edwards Air Force Base, California 5. Folsum, California 6. a. Tucson, Arizona b. Bisbee, Arizona 7. Springfield, Illinois 8. He was chaplain for the U.S. Senate in Washington, D.C. 9. Quebec, Quebec

The Miracle Worker: Anne Bancroft, Patty Duke

Dramatic Movies of the 1960's

Match the following dramas with their locations. [Expert rating = 9 out of 11]

1. **Banning**, 1967 starring Robert Wagner and Jill St. John
2. **The Cincinnati Kid**, 1965 starring Steve McQueen, Edward G. Robinson
3. **David & Lisa**, 1962 starring Keir Dullea and Janet Margolin
4. **Diamond Head**, 1962 starring Charlton Heston, Yvette Mimieux
5. **The Group**, 1966 starring Candace Bergen and Joan Hackett
6. **Inherit the Wind**, 1960 starring Spencer Tracy and Frederic March
7. **The Miracle Worker**, 1962 starring Anne Bancroft and Patty Duke
8. **Paper Lion**, 1968 starring Alan Alda, Lauren Hutton, and Alex Karras
9. **Ring of Fire**, 1961 starring David Janssen, Frank Gorshin
10. **Seven Days in May**, 1964 starring Burt Lancaster and Kirk Douglas
11. **The Slender Thread**, 1965 starring Sidney Poitier and Anne Bancroft

a. Aberdeen, Washington
b. Dayton, Tennessee
c. Detroit, Michigan
d. Honolulu, Hawaii
e. Los Angeles, California
f. New Orleans, Louisiana
g. Philadelphia, Pennsylvania
h. Poughkeepsie, New York
i. Seattle, Washington
j. Tuscumbia, Alabama
k. Washington, D.C.

Answers: 1. e 2. f 3. g 4. d 5. h 6. b 7. j 8. c 9. a 10. k 11. i

Laugh Lines at the Movies

1. Name three recent movie comedies set in Beverly Hills, California.

2. For some reason Baltimore, Maryland, has become a favorite setting for movie comedies. Can you name three recent comedies set in Baltimore?

3. Philadelphia, Pennsylvania, has also become a favorite setting for movie comedies. Name two comedies set in Philadelphia.

4. The 1969 comedy, **Alice's Restaurant**, was based on the Arlo Guthrie song of the same name. Where is Alice's restaurant?

5. Can you name the locations of the following two movies starring Jerry Lewis?

    a. **The Bellboy** (1960)

    b. **Jumping Jacks** (1952) also starring Dean Martin

6. Can you name the locations of the following movies directed by Robert Altman?

    a. **Brewster McCloud**, 1970 starring Bud Cort and Sally Kellerman

    b. **Health**, 1979 starring James Garner and Carol Burnett

---

1. Beverly Hills Cop; The Couch Trip; Down and Out in Beverly Hills; Ruthless People; Shampoo; . . .   2. Amazing Grace; And Justice for All; Clara's Heart; Hairspray; Her Alibi; St. Elmo's Fire; Tin Men   3. Mannequin; Trading Places   4. Stockbridge, Massachusetts   5. a. Miami Beach, Florida   b. Fort Benning, Georgia   6. a. Houston, Texas   b. Saint Petersburg, Florida

Other Movie Comedies

Can you match the following movie comedies with their locations? [Expert rating: 10 out of 13]

1. **The Adventures of Tom Sawyer**, 1938 starring Tommy Kelly, Jackie Moran

2. **Born Yesterday**, 1950 starring Judy Holliday and William Holden

3. **Bus Stop**, 1956 starring Marilyn Monroe and Don Murray

4. **Car Wash**, 1976 starring Richard Pryor, Franklyn Ajaye, Sully Boyar

5. **Disorderlies**, 1987 comedy starring the Fat Boys and Ralph Bellamy

6. **Foolin' Around**, 1980 starring Gary Busey and Annette O'Toole

7. **The Fortune Cookie**, 1966 starring Jack Lemmon and Walter Matthau

8. **Harry and the Hendersons**, 1986 starring John Lithgow, Melinda Dillon

9. **Jitterbugs**, 1943 starring Stan Laurel and Oliver Hardy

10. **Play It Again, Sam**, 1972 starring Woody Allen and Diane Keaton

11. **Russians Are Coming, Russians Are Coming**, 1966 starring Alan Arkin

12. **Sky Full of Moon**, 1952 starring Carleton Carpenter and Jan Sterling

13. **Tough Guys Don't Dance**, 1987 crime drama starring Ryan O'Neal

a. Cleveland, Ohio
b. Hannibal, Missouri
c. Las Vegas, Nevada
d. Los Angeles, California
e. Nantucket, Massachusetts
f. New Orleans, Louisiana
g. Palm Beach, Florida
h. Phoenix, Arizona
i. Provincetown, Massachusetts
j. Saint Paul, Minnesota
k. San Francisco, California
l. Seattle, Washington
m. Washington, D.C.

Answers: 1. b   2. m   3. h   4. d   5. g   6. j   7. a   8. l   9. f   10. k   11. e   12. c   13. i

The Movie Westerns

Here are some of the more famous westerns (and a few not so famous). Can you match these westerns with their locations? Note that several choices are used twice. [Expert rating: 10 out of 13]

1. **Ace High,** 1969 starring Terrance Hill and Eli Wallach
2. **The Alamo,** 1960 starring John Wayne and Richard Widmark
3. **Barbary Coast,** 1935 starring Miriam Hopkins and Edward G. Robinson
4. **City of Bad Men,** 1953 starring Jeanne Crain and Dale Robertson
5. **Gunfight at the OK Corral,** 1957 starring Burt Lancaster and Kirk Douglas
6. **The Life and Times of Judge Roy Bean,** 1972 starring Paul Newman
7. **Maverick Queen,** 1956 starring Barbara Stanwyck and Barry Sullivan
8. **My Darling Clementine,** 1946 starring Henry Fonda and Victor Mature
9. **Once Upon a Texas Train,** 1986 TV movie
10. **Red Tomahawk,** 1967 starring Howard Keel and Broderick Crawford
11. **The Shootist,** 1976 starring John Wayne, Lauren Bacall, James Stewart
12. **The Texas Rangers,** 1936 starring Fred MacMurray and Jackie Oakie
13. **True Grit,** 1969 starring John Wayne, Glen Campbell, and Kim Darby

a. Carson City, Nevada
b. Carson City, Nevada
c. Deadwood, South Dakota
d. Del Rio, Texas
e. El Paso, Texas
f. Langtry, Texas
g. Laredo, Texas
h. Montrose, Colorado
i. Rock Springs, Wyoming
j. San Antonio, Texas
k. San Francisco, California
l. Tombstone, Arizona
m. Tombstone, Arizona

Answers: 1. e   2. j   3. k   4. a / b   5. l / m   6. f   7. i   8. l / m   9. d   10. c   11. a / b   12. g   13. h

Dramatic Movies of the 1970's

Can you match the following movie dramas of the 1970's with the locations in which they were set? [Expert rating = 8 out of 10]

1. **American Graffiti**, 1973 starring Richard Dreyfuss and Ron Howard
2. **And Justice for All**, 1979 starring Al Pacino, Jack Warden, John Forsythe
3. **The Apprenticeship of Duddy Kravitz**, 1974 starring Richard Dreyfuss
4. **Black Sunday**, 1977 starring Robert Shaw and Bruce Dern
5. **Breaking Away**, 1979 starring Dennis Christopher and Dennis Quaid
6. **The Brinks Job**, 1978 starring Peter Falk, Peter Boyle, Warren Oates
7. **The China Syndrome**, 1979 starring Jack Lemmon and Jane Fonda
8. **Chinatown**, 1974 starring Jack Nicholson and Faye Dunaway
9. **Conrack**, 1974 starring Jon Voight, Paul Winfield, Madge Sinclair
10. **The Deer Hunter**, 1978 starring Robert DeNiro, John Cazale, John Savage

a. Baltimore, Maryland
b. Bloomington, Indiana
c. Boston, Massachusetts
d. Clairton, Pennsylvania
e. Los Angeles, California
f. Miami, Florida
g. Modesto, California
h. Montreal, Quebec
i. Saint Simons Island, Georgia
j. Ventana, California

Answers: 1. g 2. a 3. h 4. f 5. b 6. c 7. j 8. e 9. i 10. d

More Dramatic Movies of the 1970's

Match the following movie dramas with the locations in which they were set? [Expert rating = 8 out of 11]

1. **The Paper Chase**, 1973 starring Timothy Bottoms and John Houseman
2. **Play Misty for Me**, 1971 starring Clint Eastwood and Jessica Walter
3. **Pretty Baby**, 1978 starring Brooke Shields and Keith Carradine
4. **Pursuit**, 1972 TV movie starring Ben Gazzara
5. **The Sting**, 1973 starring Paul Newman, Robert Redford, Robert Shaw
6. **Taxi Driver**, 1976 starring Robert DeNiro and Cybill Shepherd
7. **The Town That Dreaded Sundown**, 1977 starring Ben Johnson
8. **The Turning Point**, 1977 starring Shirley MacLaine and Anne Bancroft
9. **W W & the Dixie Dance Kings**, 1975 starring Burt Reynolds, Art Carney
10. **Walking Tall**, 1973 starring Joe Don Baker and Elizabeth Hartman
11. **Welcome to Arrow Beach**, 1977 starring Laurence Harvey, Joanna Pettit

a. Cambridge, Massachusetts
b. Chicago, Illinois
c. Monterey, California
d. Nashville, Tennessee
e. New Orleans, Louisiana
f. New York, New York
g. Oklahoma City, Oklahoma
h. San Diego, California
i. Santa Barbara, California
j. Selma, Tennessee
k. Texarkana, Texas

Answers: 1. a   2. c   3. e   4. h   5. b   6. f   7. k   8. g   9. d   10. j   11. i

Play Misty For Me: Clint Eastwood, Jessica Walter © Universal Pictures / Shooting Star

Action Movies and Crime Stories

1. San Francisco has become a popular location for police and detective movies. Name three recent such movies set in San Francisco.

2. New Orleans has also become a popular setting for detective and action dramas. Name three recent dramas set in New Orleans.

3. Name two recent action movies set in Detroit, Michigan.

4. Name three crime movies set in Chicago.

1. Big Trouble in Little China; Bullitt; Burglar; Dirty Harry; The Enforcer; 48 Hours; Foul Play; Jagged Edge; Magnum Force; Sudden Impact

2. Angel Heart; The Big Easy; No Mercy; Tightrope

3. Action Jackson; Robocop; also the beginnings of both Beverly Hills Cop movies

4. Above the Law; Call Northside 777; Capone; Chicago Confidential; Chicago Syndicate; City That Never Sleeps, Code of Silence; Red Heat; Running Scared; The Saint Valentine's Day Massacre; The Sting; The Untouchables

More Action Movies and Crime Stories

Match the following movies with the town in which they were located. Note that Seattle is used as a setting for two of the movies. [Expert rating = 7 out of 10]

1. **Bridge Across Time**, 1985 starring David Hasselhoff and Stepfanie Kramer
2. **City Heat**, 1984 starring Clint Eastwood and Burt Reynolds
3. **French Connection**, 1971, Gene Hackman, Fernando Rey, Roy Scheider
4. **Plain Clothes**, 1988 starring Arliss Howard, Suzy Amis, Diane Ladd
5. **Squad Car**, 1960 starring Vici Raaf, Paul Bryar, Don Marlowe
6. **Tony Rome**, 1967 starring Frank Sinatra and Jill St. John
7. **Harbor Lights**, 1964 starring Kent Taylor, Jeff Morrow, Miriam Colon
8. **The Raid** , 1954 historical action starring Van Heflin and Richard Boone
9. **Seven**, 1979 action movie starring William Smith and Barbara Leigh
10. **Stakeout**, 1987 starring Richard Dreyfuss and Emilio Estevez

a. Honolulu, Hawaii
b. Kansas City, Missouri
c. Lake Havasu City, Arizona
d. Miami, Florida
e. New York, New York
f. Phoenix, Arizona
g. Saint Albans, Vermont
h. San Juan, Puerto Rico
i. Seattle, Washington
j. Seattle, Washington

Answers: 1. c   2. b   3. e   4. i / j   5. f   6. d   7. h   8. g   9. a   10. i / j

Movie Dramas of the 1980's

Can you name the locations of the following 1980's movie dramas? [Expert rating: 9 out of 12]

1. **Absence of Malice**, 1981 starring Paul Newman and Sally Fields
2. **The Big Easy**, 1987 starring Dennis Quaid and Ellen Barkin
3. **Bombs Away**, 1985 starring Micahel Huddleston and Pat McCormick
4. **The Breakfast Club**, 1985 starring Molly Ringwald and Judd Nelson
5. **Deathtrap**, 1982 starring Michael Caine and Christopher Reeve
6. **The Dollmaker**, 1984 starring Jane Fonda and Levon Helm
7. **Flying Blind**, 1988 starring Richard Panebianco
8. **Hoosiers**, 1986 starring Gene Hackman and Dennis Hopper
9. **Ironweed**, 1987 starring Jack Nicholson and Meryl Streep
10. **The Karate Kid**, 1985 starring Pat Morita and Ralph Macchio
11. **Light of Day**, 1986 starring Michael J. Fox and Joan Jett
12. **The Manhattan Project**, 1985 starring Christopher Collet, Cynthia Nixon

a. Albany, New York
b. Cleveland, Ohio
c. Detroit, Michigan
d. East Hampton, Connecticut
e. Ithaca, New York
f. Miami, Florida
g. Milan, Indiana
h. New Orleans, Louisiana
i. Northbrook, Illinois
j. Philadelphia, Pennsylvania
k. Reseda, California
l. Seattle, Washington

Answers: 1. f   2. h   3. l   4. i   5. d   6. c   7. j   8. g   9. a   10. k   11. b   12. e

More Movie Dramas of the 1980's

Here are a few more movie dramas of the 1980's. Can you match the following movies with their locations? [Expert rating: 9 out of 13]

1. **Marie: A True Story**, 1985 starring Sissy Spacek and Jeff Daniels
2. **The Mean Season**, 1985 starring Kurt Russell and Mariel Hemingway
3. **Miracle on Ice**, 1981 TV movie starring Karl Malden
4. **A Night in the Life of Jimmy Rearden**, 1988 starring River Phoenix
5. **The Outsiders**, 1985 starring Matt Dillon, Ralph Macchio, Rob Lowe
6. **Over the Top**, 1987 starring Sylvester Stallone, Robert Loggia
7. **Power**, 1986 starring Richard Gere, Julie Christie, Gene Hackman
8. **The Right Stuff**, 1983 space drama starring Sam Shepard and Scott Glenn
9. **Square Dance**, 1987 starring Jason Robards and Jane Alexander
10. **Target**, 1985 starring Gene Hackman, Matt Dillon, Gayle Hunnicutt
11. **Vision Quest**, 1985 starring Matthew Modine and Linda Fiorentino
12. **White of the Eye**, 1987 starring Cathy Moriarty and David Keith
13. **The Woman in Red**, 1984 starring Gene Wilder and Kelly LeBrock

a. Dallas, Texas
b. Evanston, Illinois
c. Fort Worth, Texas
d. Houston, Texas
e. Knoxville, Tennessee
f. Lake Placid, New York
g. Las Vegas, Nevada
h. Miami, Florida
i. San Francisco, California
j. Santa Fe, New Mexico
k. Spokane, Washington
l. Tucson, Arizona
m. Tulsa, Oklahoma

Answers: 1. e   2. h   3. f   4. b   5. m   6. g   7. j   8. d   9. c   10. a   11. k   12. l   13. i

Movies of 1987

Here are some more movies from 1987. Can you match the following movies with their settings? [Expert rating: 9 out of 13]

1. **The Bedroom Window**, starring Steve Guttenberg, Elizabeth McGovern
2. **Bell Diamond**, drama starring Marshall Caddis and Sarah Wyss
3. **Can't Buy Me Love**, romance starring Patrick Dempsey, Amanda Peterson
4. **Concrete Angels**, teen drama starring Joseph Dimambro, Luke McKeehan
5. **Extreme Prejudice**, action story starring Nick Nolte, Powers Boothe
6. **Fire and Ice**, romance starring John Eaves, Suzy Chaffee, John Denver
7. **Heat**, crime drama starring Burt Reynolds and Karen Young
8. **Lady Beware**, drama starring Diane Lane and Michael Woods
9. **The Lost Boys**, horror comedy starring Jason Patric and Corey Haim
10. **Orphans**, drama starring Albert Finney, Matthew Modine, Kevin Anderson
11. **Raising Arizona**, starring Holly Hunter and Nicholas Cage
12. **Russkies**, comedy adventure starring Whip Hubley and Leaf Phoenix
13. **Wall Street**, drama starring Michael Douglas and Charlie Sheen

a. Aspen, Colorado
b. Baltimore, Maryland
c. Butte, Montana
d. El Paso, Texas
e. Key West, Florida
f. Las Vegas, Nevada
g. New York, New York
h. Newark, New Jersey
i. Pittsburgh, Pennsylvania
j. Santa Cruz, California
k. Tempe, Arizona
l. Toronto, Ontario
m. Tucson, Arizona

Answers: 1. b   2. c   3. m   4. l   5. d   6. a   7. f   8. i   9. j   10. h   11. k   12. e   13. g

38

Movies of 1988

Here are some movies from 1988 (and perhaps beyond). Can you match the following movies with their settings? [Expert rating: 9 out of 13]

1. **Acting School**, drama starring Morgan Freeman
2. **Bright Lights, Big City**, drama starring Michael J. Fox, Kiefer Sutherland
3. **Colors**, drama starring Robert Duvall and Sean Penn
4. **D.O.A.**, murder mystery starring Dennis Quaid
5. **Dominick & Eugene**, drama starring Tom Hulce and Ray Liotta
6. **Major League**, drama starring Tom Berenger and Charlie Sheen
7. **Night Zoo**, drama starring Gilles Maheu
8. **Pass the Ammo**, coming soon to a theatre near you
9. **The Presidio**, drama starring Mark Harmon, Sean Connery, and Meg Ryan
10. **Red Heat**, crime drama starring Arnold Schwarzenegger and Jim Belushi
11. **Shag**, drama starring Phoebe Cates
12. **You Dropped It, You Pick It Up**, coming soon to a theatre near you
13. **Young Guns**, western starring Charlie Sheen, Emilio Estevez, others

a. Austin, Texas
b. Chicago, Illinois
c. Cleveland Ohio
d. Lebanon, Tennessee
e. Little Rock, Arkansas
f. Los Angeles, California
g. Montreal, Quebec
h. Myrtle Beach, South Carolina
i. New York, New York
j. Paterson, New Jersey
k. Pittsburgh, Pennsylvania
l. San Francisco, California
m. Santa Fe, New Mexico

Answers: 1. j 2. i 3. f 4. a 5. k 6. c 7. g 8. e 9. l 10. b 11. h 12. d 13. m

Science Fiction Movies and Thrillers

1. One of the classic science fiction movies of the 1950's was **The Blob,** starring Steve McQueen. What town was the setting for this movie?

2. Steve McQueen also starred in the 1974 movie, **The Towering Inferno,** the disaster movie to end all disaster movies. Where was the towering inferno located?

3. In **Star Trek IV: The Voyage Home,** the crew of the Starship Enterprise returned to the past (in our time) to save Earth. To what city did they return?

4. The 1986 movie, **Howard the Duck,** featured the adventures of an alien, but lovable, duck-like creature who, through a cosmic coincidence, ended up here on Earth. What American city did he fall into?

5. Sydney Penny, Ricky Paull Goldin, and Kennan Wynn starred in the 1986 science fiction movie, **Hyper Sapien: People from Another Star.** While the movie was shot in western Canada, it was set near a city in the western United States. Which city?

6. **The Boy Who Could Fly** was a 1986 romantic fantasy starring Lucy Deakins, Jay Underwood, and Fred Savage. The movie was set in what Canadian city?

7. The 1972 sequel, **Conquest of the Planet of the Apes** (starring Roddy McDowall, Don Murray, and Ricardo Montalban), of the science fiction classic, **Planet of the Apes,** used the futuristic buildings of a university campus for some of the scenes. What university campus was featured, and where is it located?

8. While the 1954 classic creature feature, **The Creature from the Black Lagoon,** was set in the Amazon River valley, it was actually filmed in the United States. Where was it filmed?

9. The first **Tarzan** movie, starring Elmo Lincoln, was made in 1917. Where was it filmed?

10. **Zadar! Cow From Hell!,** a new comedy produced by the Duck's Breath Mystery Theatre, is about a Hollywood movie crew that comes to the fictitious town of Howdy, Iowa, to make a horror film about a giant, irradiated cow. Where was the film actually shot?

11. The 1963 Alfred Hitchcock thriller, **The Birds,** was filmed in what California seaside community?

12. Can you name the locations of the following five thrillers?

　　a. **The Beast Within,** a 1982 horror movie starring Ronny Cox and Bibi Besch.

　　b. **Coma,** the 1978 medical mystery thriller starring Genevieve Bujold and Michael Douglas.

　　c. **The Seventh Sign,** the 1988 thriller starring Demi Moore and Michael Biehn.

　　d. **Shadow of a Doubt,** the 1943 Alfred Hitchcock thriller about a Merry Widow murderer starring Joseph Cotton, Teresa Wright, Hume Cronyn, and Macdonald Carey

　　e. **Together Brothers,** a 1974 suspense movie about five young blacks searching for the killer of their policeman friend. Among the stars were Ahmad Nurradin, Anthony Wilson, Nelson Sims, Kenneth Bell, Owen Pace, and Kim Dorsey.

1. Chester Springs, Pennsylvania 2. San Francisco, California 3. San Francisco, California 4. Cleveland, Ohio 5. Cheyenne, Wyoming
6. Vancouver, British Columbia 7. University of California at Irvine; Irvine, California 8. Wakulla Springs State Park, outside Crawfordville, Florida
9. Morgan City, Louisiana 10. Iowa City, Iowa 11. Bodega Bay, California
12. a. Jackson, Mississippi b. Boston, Massachusetts c. Venice, California d. Santa Rosa, California e. Galveston, Texas

Hometowns

Movie characters don't live in a vacuum. They have a past. Do you know the "hometowns" of the following movie characters?

1. What was the hometown of the two women (played by Jane Russell and Marilyn Monroe) in the 1953 hit, **Gentleman Prefer Blondes**?

2. For what team did Brewster (Richard Pryor) pitch for in the 1985 comedy, **Brewster's Millions**?

3. What were the hometowns of the following two male dancers, John Phillips and Tornado, in the 1981 TV movie, **For Ladies Only**?

4. What was the hometown of Eli Mackernutt (Michael Link), the boy who was a **Stowaway to the Moon** in the 1975 TV movie?

5. Sidney Poitier played Virgil Tubbs, a city detective transplanted to a small town in the 1967 movie, **In the Heat of the Night**. Mr. Tubbs came from what city?

6. In the movie, **Indiscretion**, Jennifer Jones plays an American housewife who falls in love with a college professor in Italy. What was her hometown?

7. In the 1980 comedy, **Private Benjamin**, Goldie Hawn played the lead character. What was Private Benjamin's hometown?

8. Where were the hometowns of Tom Tuttle (John Candy) and Lawrence Bourne III (Tom Hanks) in the 1985 comedy, **Volunteers**?

9. The 1986 comedy takeoff of **Dragnet** begins with Sergeant Joe Friday (Dan Ackroyd) learning that his partner has retired. Where did his former partner move to? And what is his new hobby?

10. What is the hometown of Glenn Miller (James Stewart) in the 1954 biographical movie, **The Glenn Miller Story?**

11. In the 1980 comedy, **The Private Eyes**, what was the hometown of Doctor Tart (Tim Conway)?

12. Nadia Gates (Kim Basinger) was Bruce Willis's **Blind Date** in the 1987 comedy of the same name. What southern city was Nadia's hometown?

13. Eddie Murphy played a military tank instructor in the 1984 comedy, **Best Defense**. Where was his hometown?

14. In the 1986 hit, **Beverly Hills Cop**, Eddie Murphy plays a police detective from what city?

15. In the 1985 adventure movie, **Gotcha**, Linda Fiorentino plays a CIA spy code-named Sasha Banacek (real name Cheryl Brewster). What was her hometown?

16. In the 1984 comedy, **Basic Training**, Ann Dusenberg plays a Pentagon secretary named Melinda Griffith who later becomes Secretary of Defense. What Ohio town was her hometown?

17. What were the hometowns of the three main characters (played by William Hurt, Holly Hunter, and Albert Brooks) in the 1987 romantic comedy, **Broadcast News**?

1. Little Rock, Arkansas 2. The Hackensack Bulls of Hackensack, New Jersey 3. Iowa City, Iowa, and Wichita, Kansas 4. Titusville, Florida 5. Philadelphia, Pennsylvania 6. Philadelphia, Pennsylvania 7. Philadelphia, Pennsylvania 8. Tacoma, Washington, and Darien, Connecticut 9. Ukiah, California; raising chickens 10. Clarinda, Iowa 11. Saint Paul, Minnesota 12. Baton Rouge, Louisiana 13. Cleveland, Ohio 14. Detroit, Michigan 15. Pittsburgh, Pennsylvania 16. Ashtabula, Ohio 17. Kansas City, Kansas; Atlanta, Georgia; and Boston, Massachusetts

Passing Through

In some movies, the characters end up travelling from one town to another. Can you name some of the towns and cities the following characters pass through during their movie adventures?

1. In the 1985 comedy, **Lost in America**, Albert Brooks and Julie Hagerty play a professional couple who move from Los Angeles to New York. Can you name any of the towns and cities they passed through while driving cross country in an RV?

2. In the 1972 Neil Simon movie, **The Heartbreak Kid**, Charles Grodin plays a newly-married man who deserts his wife for another woman (Cybill Shepherd). Where is he from? Where did he go for his honeymoon? And where did he go with the other women to meet her parents?

3. Jack Nicholson plays a sailor escorting another sailor to the brig in the 1973 comedy-drama, **The Last Detail**. What cities did they pass through on their way to the brig.

4. In the 1947 romance, **The Homestretch**, Cornel Wilde plays a horse-owner in love with Maureen O'Hara. What famous horse-racing towns does he visit during the movie?

5. Charles Bronson plays a secret service agent who has to guard the president's wife (played by his wife, Jill Ireland) in the 1987 adventure movie, **Assassination**. In traveling from the east coast to the west coast, what cities did they pass through?

6. James Brolin plays Clayton Davis, an independent trucker, in the 1978 TV movie, **Steel Cowboy**. Name some of the cities he trucks to and from.

7. In the 1971 TV movie, **The Catcher**, Michael Witney and Jan-Michael Vincent play detectives who hunt down missing persons. Michael plays Noah Hendricks, an ex-cop from what city? Jan-Michael plays a graduate of what university? Also, name some of the cities they visit during their trips to locate errant husbands and other missing persons.

8. In the 1984 movie, **Fandango**, Judd Hirsch and Kevin Costner play recent college graduates who go on one last fling before settling down to real life. Can you name the three Texas towns they pass through on their way to dig up a buried bottle of champagne? At the end of the movie, they hire a doped-out pilot to fly to a large Texas city to pick up the bride for their friend's wedding. What two cities does the pilot pass through on the way to picking up the bride?

9. In the 1987 movie, **Planes, Trains, and Automobiles**, Steve Martin and John Candy play two men traveling by plane from New York to Chicago. Name some of the cities they end up in during their trip by plane, train, and automobile.

1. Las Vegas, Nevada - Boulder City, Nevada - Safford, Arizona - Houston, Texas - New Orleans, Louisiana - Mobile, Alabama - Atlanta, Georgia - Washington, DC 2. New York, New York; Miami, Florida; Minneapolis, Minnesota 3. Norfolk, Virginia - Washington, DC - New York, New York - Portsmouth, New Hampshire 4. Louisville, Kentucky - Hialeah, Florida - Saratoga Springs, New York 5. Washington, DC - Gettysburg, Pennsylvania - Kokomo, Indiana - Laramie, Wyoming - Tahoe City, California - Newport Beach, California 6. Amarillo, Texas - Bakersfield, California - Bend, Oregon - Chicago, Illinois 7. Seattle, Washington; Harvard University, Cambridge, Massachusetts; Atlanta, Georgia - Dothan, Alabama - Hot Springs, Arkansas - Nashville, Tennessee 8. Marfa, Texas - Pecos, Texas - Presidio, Texas; Cleveland, Texas - Houston, Texas 9. Chicago, Illinois - New York, New York - Saint Louis, Missouri - Wichita, Kansas

To and From Movies

These movies started in one town and ended in another. Name the towns. [Expert: 10 out of 14]

1. **The Big Bus**, 1976 disaster spoof starring Stockard Channing and Joseph Bologna
2. **The Buddy Holly Story**, 1978 biography starring Gary Busey
3. **Fraternity Vacation**, 1985 comedy starring Stephen Geoffreys and Sheree Wilson
4. **The Gauntlet**, 1977 drama starring Clint Eastwood and Sandra Locke
5. **Hijack!**, 1973 TV movie starring David Janssen and Keenan Wynn
6. **I Married Wyatt Earp**, 1986 TV movie
7. **La Bamba**, 1987 biography of Ritchie Valens starring Lou Diamond Phillips
8. **Let's Do It Again**, 1975 comedy starring Sidney Poitier and Bill Cosby
9. **The Narrow Margin**, 1952 drama starring Charles McGraw and Marie Windsor
10. **North by Northwest**, 1959 drama starring Cary Grant and Eva Marie Saint
11. **Outrageous Fortune**, 1986 comedy starring Bette Midler and Shelley Long
12. **The Remarkable Mr. Pennypacker**, 1959 drama starring Clifton Webb and Dorothy McGuire
13. **Vanishing Point**, 1971 car chase starring Barry Newman
14. **Witness**, 1985 drama starring Harrison Ford and Kelly McGillis

1. New York, New York - Denver, Colorado 2. Lubbock, Texas - Clear Lake, Iowa 3. Des Moines, Iowa - Palm Springs, California 4. Las Vegas, Nevada - Phoenix, Arizona 5. Los Angeles, California - Houston, Texas 6. Colma, California - Tombstone, Arizona 7. Pacoima, Californa - Clear Lake, Iowa 8. Atlanta, Georgia - New Orleans, Louisiana 9. Chicago, Illinois - Los Angeles, California 10. New York, New York - Mount Rushmore, South Dakota 11. New York, New York - Albuquerque, New Mexico 12. Harrisburg, Pennsylvania - Philadelphia, Pennsylvania 13. Denver, Colorado - San Francisco, California 14. Philadelphia, Pennsylvania - Lancaster, Pennsylvania

Destinations

1. What was the destination of Ryan and Tatum O'Neal in the 1973 movie, **Paper Moon?**

2. What small town was the destination of the cattle drive in the 1972 John Wayne western, **The Cowboys?**

3. And the destination for the cattle drive in the 1948 John Wayne classic, **Red River?**

4. Arlo Pear (Richard Pryor) was moving from the New Jersey suburbs to what town in the 1988 comedy, **Moving?**

5. What was the destination of the Griswold family (played by Chevy Chase and Beverly D'Angelo) in the 1983 comedy, **National Lampoon's Vacation?**

6. Speaking of vacations, in the 1986 detective comedy, **Running Scared**, where did the two Chicago policemen (starring Gregory Hines and Billy Crystal) go for their vacation?

1. Saint Joseph, Missouri 2. Belle Fourche, South Dakota 3. Abilene, Texas 4. Boise, Idaho 5. Walleyworld (a takeoff on Disneyland in Anaheim, California) 6. Key West, Florida

Misdirection

Some movies tell the story of one city or town but were actually filmed in another city. Or, in some other cases, the title of the movie seems to indicate that the movie is set in one city when it is actually set in another. Do you know where the following movies were filmed or located?

1. Where was the first movie western (1903), **The Great Train Robbery**, shot?

2. The 1986 drama, **Hoosiers**, told the story of the 1954 Indiana high school basketball champions from Milan, Indiana. Where was the movie filmed?

3. **Amazing Grace** was a 1974 comedy about corrupt politicians in Baltimore, Maryland. Where was the movie made?

4. What was the location for the 1965 drama, **The Cincinnati Kid**, starring Steve McQueen?

5. The 1954 historical drama starring Dale Robertson, **The Gambler from Natchez**, is set in what city?

6. The 1955 western starring James Stewart, **The Man from Laramie**, tells the story of a man hunting down the killers of his brother. In what state does he hunt them down?

7. The 1986 TV movie, **I Married Wyatt Earp**, started in Colma, California, and ended in Tombstone, Arizona. In what two cities was the movie shot?

8. The 1947 movie, **Boomerang**, dramatized the true story of an unsolved murder of a priest in Bridgeport, Connecticut. Where was the movie made?

9. **Tess of the Storm Country** was a 1961 drama about a Scottish girl and her uncle settling down in the Pennsylvania Dutch country. Where was this movie filmed?

10. The 1959 comedy, **Some Like It Hot,** starred Tony Curtis and Jack Lemmon as two musicians who join an all-girl band (with Marilyn Monroe) to avoid gangsters. The movie was set in Miami, Florida. Where was it filmed?

11. The 1988 **Baby M** TV miniseries, starring JoBeth Williams and John Shea as the Sterns (of Tenafly, New Jersey), tells the story of the famous surrogate mother case tried at the Bergen County courthouse in Hackensack, New Jersey. Where was this miniseries filmed?

12. The 1987 detective romance, **Stakeout** (starring Richard Dreyfuss and Emilio Estavez) is set in Seattle, Washington. Where was it filmed?

13. The 1988 movie, **Tucker: The Man and His Dream,** relates the biography of Preston Tucker, the man who designed the Tucker automobile. While his true hometown was Ypsilanti, Michigan, the movie was filmed in what locations?

14. While the 1987 TV murder mystery movie, **Laguna Heat,** was set in Laguna Beach, Santa Ana, and Newport Beach, California, most of the movie was shot in what other California cities?

15. While the Hindenburg dirigible disaster actually occurred in Lakehurst, New Jersey, the 1975 film, **The Hindenburg,** substituted a Marine Corp Air Station in what city?

1. Dover, New Jersey 2. Nineveh, Indiana 3. Philadelphia, Pennsylvania 4. New Orleans, Louisiana 5. New Orleans, Louisiana 6. New Mexico 7. Old Tucson, Arizona, and Phoeniz, Arizona 8. Stamford, Connecticut 9. Sonora, California 10. Coronado, California 11. Van Nuys, California and Secaucus, New Jersey 12. Vancouver, British Columbia 13. Sonoma, California, and other locations around Oakland, California 14. Los Angeles and Oxnard, California 15. Tustin, California

Movies — On Location

1. Where was the 1980 comedy, **The Private Eyes** (starring Don Knotts and Tim Conway) filmed?

2. Jane Fonda's latest movie, **Union Street**, was shot in what two cities? Which city passed a resolution opposing her plans to shoot scenes in the city because of her Vietnam War activities?

3. Paul Newman directed his wife, Joanne Woodward, in the 1972 drama, **The Effect of Gamma Rays on Man-in-the-Moon Marigolds**. Where was this movie filmed?

4. The 1987 movie, **Farm of the Year**, was filmed at what two locations?

5. Don Johnson's new movie, **Sweatheart's Dance**, was filmed in what small New England town?

6. The controversial 1987 TV miniseries, **Amerika**, was filmed in what midwest town?

7. Besides location shots in Washington, DC, and Tunisia, what California town was used for filming the 1984 Goldie Hawn comedy, **Protocol**?

8. Sam Shepard's latest movie, **Far North**, was shot on a farm outside what midwestern city?

9. Stephen King's horror novel, **The Shining** (starring Jack Nicholson), was filmed where?

10. Two of Clint Eastwood's recent westerns, **The Outlaw Josey Wales** and **Pale Rider**, were made in what California location?

11. The 1938 Errol Flynn movie, The Adventures of Robin Hood, was located in England but shot in California. Where was it filmed?

12. The 1984 comedy, **Up the Creek**, starring Tim Matheson and Jennifer Runyon, was filmed at what Pacific Northwest location?

13. The 1985 romantic comedy, **Paradise Motel**, starred Gary Hershberger and Jonna Leigh Stack. Where was the Paradise Motel located?

14. Name three of the locations used for the Peter Seller comedy, **Being There**.

15. The 1988 movie, **Someone to Love**, was filmed in a movie theater in what city?

16. The 1955 John Wayne movie about Genghis Khan, **The Conqueror**, was filmed where?

17. While the 1960 John Wayne movie, **The Alamo**, is set in San Antonio, it was actually filmed at the western movie set, Alamo Village. Where is Alamo Village located?

18. For the 1939 movie, **Arizona**, Columbia Pictures built its own western set, which has since been used for many other movies, including **Three Amigos!** and **Cannonball Run II**. Where is it?

19. James Dean's last movie, the 1956 drama **Giant**, also starred Elizabeth Taylor and Rock Hudson. Where was this movie filmed?

20. **Johnny Be Good**, the 1988 comedy starring Anthony Michael Hall, was filmed in what two Texas towns?

1. Asheville, North Carolina   2. Waterbury, Connecticut, and Holyoke, Massachusetts; Holyoke passed a resolution against "Hanoi Jane"
3. Bridgeport, Connecticut   4. The farm was shot at Worthington, Iowa; the Jones County Fair was shot at Monticello, Iowa.   5. Hyde Park, Vermont
6. Tecumseh, Nebraska   7. Auburn, California   8. Duluth, Minnesota   9. Estes Park, Colorado   10. Oroville, California   11. Chicao, California
(the archery contest was at Busch Gardens in Pasadena, California)   12. Bend, Oregon   13. Norwalk, California   14. Washington, D.C.; Pasadena, California; and Asheville, North Carolina (the Biltmore mansion)   15. Santa Monica, California   16. in the Escalante Desert and Snow Canyon State Park near St. George, Utah   17. Brackettville, Texas   18. Old Tucson, Arizona   19. Marfa, Texas   20. San Antonio, Texas; Alamo Heights, Texas

More Locations

1. Texas has always been a popular location for shooting movies. Can you name at least ten other movies (besides **The Alamo, Giant,** and **Johnny Be Good**) that have been filmed in the state of Texas in the last ten years?

2. One building in New York City, however, has probably had more movies filmed within it than the whole state of Texas — over 200. Indeed, according to a recent *USA Today* article, there is at least one shooting (for commercials, TV shows, or movies) in the building every week. Can you name that building?

3. Can you name a few of the more recent movies which have used this hotel for location shooting?

4. Another building that has been used in many movies is the old Orange County Courthouse. Where is it located?

5. Name a few of the movies filmed there.

6. What Kansas town has a replica of Dorothy's house (from the 1939 classic, **The Wizard of Oz**)?

1. The Ballad of Gregorio Cortez; Barbarosa; Best Little Whorehouse in Texas; Blood Simple; The Border; Fandango; The Last Picture Show; Local Hero; The Man Who Loved Women; Nadine; 1918; Paris, Texas; Places in the Heart; Raggedy Man; Robocop; Silkwood; Tender Mercies; A Trip to Bountiful; True Stories; Urban Cowboy   2. the Plaza Hotel   3. Arthur; Barefoot in the Park; Big Business; Crocodile Dundee; Funny Girl; North by Northwest; Plaza Suite   4. Santa Ana, California   5. Compulsion; Norma Rae; Gideon's Trumpet; Frances   6. Liberal, Kansas

Orange County Locations

Since it is right next door to Los Angeles County, Orange County has often been used as a location for movies. Can you name the cities which were used as settings for the following movies?

1. What was the first movie filmed in Orange County? And where was it filmed?
2. The trenches and barbed-wire battlefields of 1930 war classic, **All Quiet on the Wester Front**, were actually located in what Orange County community?
3. When Theda Bara went floating on her barge in the 1917 version of **Cleopatra**, what bay served as the coastline of Greece?
4. For the 1921 version of **The Three Musketeers**, starring Douglas Fairbanks, where did they build the replica of the French fort?
5. In the 1954 classic, **Rebel Without a Cause**, James Dean participates in a "chicken" race which results in one car going over a cliff. Where was that cliff actually located?
6. What location served as the Sinai peninsula in the 1923 Cecil B. DeMille classic, **The Ten Commandments**?
7. The 1942 melodrama, **Juke Girl**, starring Ronald Reagan and Ann Sheridan, was filmed in the then-flourishing farm fields of what city?
8. Where were the 1937 comedy, **Topper**, and the 1943 melodrama, **Lassie Come Home**, filmed?

1. The Two Brothers; San Juan Capistrano 2. Corona del Mar 3. Upper Newport Bay in Newport Beach 4. again, in Upper Newport Bay 5. Dana Point 6. Seal Beach 7. Garden Grove 8. the Irvine Park area
[Note: Most of the information for this page came from an article, "The Back Lot" by Herman Wong, in the May 22, 1988 issue of "Celebrate!"]

The Movies Go to School

Schools have often been the setting for movies. Do you know which schools and cities were used for the location shots of the following movies?

1. Rodney Dangerfield's 1986 comedy, **Back to School**, was filmed at what university?

2. The new 1988 drama, **Heartbreak Hotel**, tells the story of a young Southern woman becoming involved in racial issues while attending a small Alabama college during the 1950's. Where was the movie filmed?

3. **Just One of the Guys** is a 1985 comedy about a girl (Joyce Hyser) going to school as a boy in order to win a journalism internship. At what high school was this film shot?

4. At what university was the beginning and end of the 1985 adventure movie, **Gotcha**, filmed?

5. The 1983 Playboy movie, **Preppies**, told the story of three prep students who were distracted from their studies by three well-endowed town girls. In what town was this movie filmed?

6. Michael J. Fox plays a werewolf in the 1985 movie, **Teen Wolf**. In what cities was it filmed?

7. Spike Lee's recent movie, **School Daze**, is set in the fictional institution of higher learning, Mission College. Where was this movie actually filmed?

1. University of Wisconsin at Madison, Wisconsin 2. University of Mississippi at Oxford, Mississippi 3. Scottsdale, Arizona high school 4. UCLA at Los Angeles, California 5. Nyack, New York 6. John Burroughs Junior High School in South Pasadena, California; also Montrose Bowling Alley in Montrose, California; also Fremont, Nebraska 7. Atlanta University in Atlanta, Georgia

Fictional and Real Towns

1. The 1986 drama, **Stand by Me,** is set in the fictional town of Castle Rock, Oregon. What town was the actual setting?

2. Aidan Quinn and Daryl Hannah starred in the 1984 drama, **Reckless,** about high school life in the mythical Everton, Ohio. Name the three towns which were used as locations for this movie.

3. The 1985 romance, **Murphy's Romance,** starring Sally Field and James Garner, was set in the fictional town of Eunice, Arizona. What town as the actual setting for the film?

4. **The Milagro Beanfield War,** the 1988 drama starring Ruben Blades and Sonia Braga, was set in fictional Milagro, New Mexico. Where was it filmed?

5. What was the name of the fictional town in the 1962 musical, **The Music Man,** starring Robert Preston and Shirley Jones?

6. And what real town was the model for this fictional town?

7. Perhaps one of the most famous fictional movie towns is Peyton Place. Where was the 1957 soap opera, **Peyton Place,** filmed?

8. The 1963 comedy, **It's a Mad, Mad, Mad, Mad World,** ended in the fictional city of Santa Rosita Beach. Where was it actually filmed?

1. Brownsville, Oregon 2. Mingo Junction, Ohio; Steubenville, Ohio; and Weirton, West Virginia 3. Florence, Arizona 4. Santa Fe and Truchas, New Mexico 5. River City 6. Mason City, Iowa 7. Camden, Maine 8. Long Beach, California

Towns as Headline Stars

Except for New York, Hollywood has received the most top billings, probably for the simple reason that Hollywood is the movie capital of the world. Here are just a few of the movies which have given Hollywood a star billing: **Boston Blackie Goes Hollywood, Going Hollywood, Hollywood Canteen, Hollywood Cavalcade, Hollywood Party, Hollywood Hotel, Hollywood or Bust, Hollywood Review of 1929, Hollywood Story, Hollywood Hot Tubs,** and **Hollywood Vice Squad.**

New York and its boroughs, however, still get the most star billings. Why? Perhaps because, as the saying goes, it is the city of a thousand stories. Here are a few of the movies featuring New York (or its boroughs) in their titles: **The Belle of New York, The Colossus of New York, The Docks of New York, The Killer That Stalked New York, King in New York, New York Town, Non-Stop New York, So This is New York, Sunday in New York, While New York Sleeps, Adventure in Manhattan, The Girl from Manhattan, Jane Austen in Manhattan, Manhattan, Manhattan Melodrama, The Muppets Take Manhattan, Romance in Manhattan, Tales of Manhattan, The Cowboy from Brooklyn, It Happened in Brooklyn, The Kid from Brooklyn**

Of other cities in the United States, Las Vegas and Chicago have gotten the most star billings, Las Vegas because of its gambling (**Crashing Las Vegas, The Las Vegas Story, Meet Me in Las Vegas, They Came to Rob Las Vegas**) and Chicago because of its crime (**Chicago Calling, Chicago Deadline, Chicago Story, Chicago Syndicate**).

Can you name some of the other cities that have been featured on the marquee? Try your memory with the movies listed on the following pages.

Towns as Stars — 1930's

This quiz is for those of you who stay up late watching old movies on TV (or at classic film festivals). Can you fill in the blanks with the names of the appropriate cities?

To aid your memory, here are the names of the cities that fill in the blanks (listed alphabetically) — Annapolis, Chicago, Dallas, New York (twice), Salem, Washington, West Point.

1. **The Duke of _____**, a 1938 drama starring Louis Hayward and Joan Fontaine

2. **_____ Farewell**, a 1935 drama starring Tom Brown and Richard Cromwell

3. **In Old _____**, a 1939 drama starring Tyrone Power, Alice Brady, and Don Ameche

4. **Maid of _____**, a 1937 drama starring Claudette Colbert and Fred MacMurray

5. **Mr. Smith Goes to _____**, a 1939 drama starring James Stewart and Jean Arthur

6. **Sidewalks of _____**, a 1931 comedy starring Buster Keaton

7. **Stella _____**, a 1937 tear-jerker starring Barbara Stanwyck (also a 1925 film starring Belle Bennett)

8. **The Toast of _____**, a 1937 drama starring Edward Arnold and Cary Grant

1. West Point, New York 2. Annapolis, Maryland 3. Chicago, Illinois 4. Salem, Massachusetts 5. Washington, D.C. 6. New York, New York
7. Dallas, Texas 8. New York, New York

Towns as Stars — 1940's

This quiz should be a little easier, so we won't give you any hints this time around. Can you fill in the blanks with the names of the appropriate cities? [Expert rating: 9 out of 14]

1. **Bells of** _____, 1947 western starring Donald Woods and Gloria Warren
2. **The Earl of** _____, 1940 drama starring Robert Montgomery and Edward Arnold
3. **The Flame of** _____, 1941 romance starring Marlene Dietrich, Bruce Cabot, and Roland Young
4. _____ **Kitty**, 1944 romance starring Joan Davis, Bob Crosby, Jane Frazee, and Erik Rolf
5. **Little Old** _____, 1940 romance starring Alice Faye, Brenda Joyce, and Fred MacMurray
6. **Meet Me in** _____, 1944 musical starring Judy Garland, Margaret O'Brien, and Mary Astor
7. **Miss Grant Takes** _____, 1949 comedy starring Lucille Ball and William Holden
8. **Moon Over** _____, 1941 musical romance Betty Grable, Don Ameche, and Bob Cummings
9. _____ **Serenade**, 1941 musical comedy starring Sonja Henie, John Payne, and Milton Berle
10. **The** _____ **Story**, 1940 romantic comedy starring Cary Grant, Katherine Hepburn, James Stewart
11. **The Streets of** _____, 1949 western starring Macdonald Carey and William Holden
12. _____ **Sue**, 1946 western starring Gene Autry and Lynne Roberts
13. _____, **The Town Too Tough to Die**, 1942 western starring Richard Dix and Edgar Buchanan
14. _____ **Trail**, 1940 western starring Errol Flynn and Olivia de Haviland

1. San Fernando, California 2. Chicago, Illinois 3. New Orleans, Louisiana 4. Kansas City, Missouri 5. New York, New York 6. Saint Louis, Missouri 7. Richmond Virginia 8. Miami, Florida 9. Sun Valley, Idaho 10. Philadelphia, Pennsylvania 11. Laredo, Texas 12. Sioux City, Iowa 13. Tombstone, Arizona 14. Santa Fe, New Mexico

Towns as Stars — 1950's

Since many of the following films don't show up as often as those in the 1940's, this quiz might be more difficult. Nonetheless, we will have no mercy. You'll still on your own. Can you fill in the blanks with the names of the appropriate cities? [Expert rating: 9 out of 11]

1. **Affair in** _____, 1957 romance starring John Lund and Doris Singleton
2. _____ **Confidential**, 1957 drama starring Brian Keith and Beverly Garland
3. **Escape from** _____, 1957 prison drama starring Johnny Desmond, Merry Anders, Richard Devon
4. **The Gambler from** _____, 1954 western starring Dale Robertson and Debra Paget
5. **Gun Duel in** _____, 1957 western starring George Montgomery and Ann Robinson
6. **The Man from** _____, 1955 western starring James Stewart and Arthur Kennedy
7. _____ **Shakedown**, 1955 drama starring Dennis O'Keefe and Coleen Gray
8. **The Spirit of** _____, 1957 drama starring James Stewart, Murray Hamilton, and Marc Connelly
9. **Those Redheads from** _____, 1953 musical starring Rhonda Fleming and Agnes Moorehead
10. **3:10 to** _____, 1957 western starring Glenn Ford and Van Heflin
11. **Toughest Gun in** _____, 1958 western starring George Montgomery and Beverly Tyler

1. Reno, Nevada 2. Chicago, Illinois 3. San Quentin, California 4. Natchez, Mississippi 5. Durango, Colorado 6. Laramie, Wyoming 7. Las Vegas, Nevada 8. Saint Louis, Missouri 9. Seattle, Washington 10. Yuma, Arizona 11. Tombstne, Arizona

Towns as Stars — 1960's

Towns weren't very popular as stars during the 1960's. To help you out with this quiz, here are the six cities that were featured as stars in the titles of these movies: Abilene, Boston, Campobello, Cincinnati, Las Vegas, Nashville. [Expert rating: 6 out of 6]

1. **From _____ with Music**, 1969 drama starring Marilyn Maxwell and Leo G. Carroll

2. **Gunfight in _____**, 1967 western starring Bobby Darin and Emily Banks

3. **The _____ Kid**, 1965 drama starring Steve McQueen, Edward G. Robinson, and Karl Malden

4. **The _____ Strangler**, 1968 drama starring Tony Curtis and Henry Fonda

5. **Sunrise at _____**, 1960 biography of Franklin Delano Roosevelt starring Ralph Bellamy and Greer Garson

6. **Viva _____**, 1964 musical romance starring Elvis Presley and Ann-Margaret

1. Nashville, Tennessee   2. Abilene, Texas   3. Cincinnati, Ohio   4. Boston, Massachusetts   5. Campobello, South Carolina   6. Las Vegas, Nevada

Towns as Stars — 1970's

Since these movies are of more recent vintage, these headliner town stars should be easier to recognize. But, if you need some help, here are your choices: Amityville, Canaan, Cheyenne, Dallas, Houston, Kansas City, Las Vegas, Los Angeles, Mobile, Northfield, Scottsboro, Washington. [Expert rating: 10 out of 12]

1. _____ **Bomber,** 1972 drama starring Raquel Welch, Kevin McCarthy, and Norman Alden
2. **A Death in** _____, 1978 TV true life drama starring Stephanie Powers and Paul Clemens
3. **The Great** _____ **Minnesota Raid,** 1972 western starring Cliff Robertson and Robert Duvall
4. **The** _____ **Horror,** 1970 horror movie starring James Brolin, Margot Kidder, and Rod Steiger
5. **Judge Horton and the** _____ **Boys,** 1976 TV true-life drama starring Arthur Hill and Vera Miles
6. _____ **Lady,** 1976 romance starring Stella Stevens and Stuart Whitman
7. **Last of the** _____ **Hot-Shots,** 1970 drama starring James Coburn and Lynn Redgrave
8. **North** _____ **Forty,** 1979 drama starring Nick Nolte and Mac Davis
9. **The** _____ **Social Club,** 1970 western starring Henry Fonda and James Stewart
10. _____, **We've Got a Problem,** 1974 TV movie starring Robert Culp, Clu Gulager, Sandra Dee
11. **Welcome to** _____, 1977 drama starring Keith Carradine and Sally Kellerman
12. **Werewolf of** _____, 1973 horror movie starring Moses Ginsburg and Dean Stockwell

1. Kansas City, Missouri 2. Canaan, Connecticut 3. Northfield, Minnesota 4. Amityville, New York 5. Scottsboro, Alabama 6. Las Vegas, Nevada 7. Mobile, Alabama 8. Dallas, Texas 9. Cheyenne, Wyoming 10. Houston, Texas 11. Los Angeles, California 12. Washington, D.C.

Towns as Stars — 1980's

You should be able to name most of these town stars without a crib sheet, but for those of you who would like some hints, the selection of towns and cities is listed after the questions (and before the answers). [Expert rating without hints: 10 out of 16; expert rating with hints: 13 out of 16]

1. The _____ **Bikini Shop**, a 1987 beach movie (actually shot in Venice, California)
2. _____ **Blues**, 1988 comedy starring Matthew Broderick and Penelope Ann Miller
3. **Born in East** _____, 1987 drama starring Cheech Marin and Paul Rodriguez
4. **The** _____ **Bullet**, 1980 drama starring James Coburn and Omar Sharif
5. _____ **Cop**, 1984 detective comedy starring Eddie Murphy and Judge Reinhold
6. _____ **Cowboy Cheerleaders II**, 1980 TV movie starring John Davidson and Laraine Stephens
7. **Doctor** _____, 1983 comedy starring Dan Aykroyd and Howard Hesseman
8. **Down and Out in** _____, 1986 comedy starring Richard Dreyfuss, Bette Midler, and Nick Nolte
9. _____ **Encounter**, 1985 true-life drama about a Texas UFO experience
10. **Escape from** _____, 1981 futuristic adventure starring Kurt Russell and Lee Van Cleef
11. **The** _____ **Experiment**, 1984 science fiction adventure starring Michael Pare and Nancy Allen

12. **The Return of the** _____ **7**, 1980 low-budget drama starring Mark Arnott, Gordon Clapp, and Maggie Cousineau

13. _____ **Lord** _____, 1989 true-life TV miniseries about the civil rights movement

14. **Slaves of** _____, 1989 drama starring Bernadette Peters and Mary Beth Hurt

15. **To Live or Die in** _____, 1985 drama starring William Petersen and Willem Dafoe

16. **A Trip to** _____, 1985 drama starring Geraldine Page and John Heard

17. _____ **Vice Squad**, 1986 police drama starring Ronny Cox and Trish Van Devere

Hints: For those of you who would like a little help, here are the names of the towns which headlined these movies: Aurora, Baltimore, Beverly Hills (twice), Biloxi, Bountiful, Dallas, Detroit, Hollywood, Los Angeles (twice), Malibu, New York (twice), Philadelphia, Secaucus, Selma

1. Malibu, California 2. Biloxi, Mississippi 3. (LA) Los Angeles, California 4. Baltimore, Maryland 5. Beverly Hills, California 6. Dallas, Texas 7. Detroit, Michigan 8. Beverly Hills, California 9. Aurora, Texas 10. New York, New York 11. Philadelphia, Pennsylvana 122. Secaucus, New Jersey 13. Selma, Alabama 14. New York, New York 15. (LA) Los Angeles, California 16. Bountiful, Utah 17. Hollywood, California

More Cities and Towns with Top Billing

Below are listed a few of the other towns that have received top billing on the movie marquee. How many do you remember?

Abilene, Texas — **Abilene Town**, 1946 western starring Randolph Scott; **Showdown at Abilene**, 1956 western starring Jock Mahoney

Albuquerque, New Mexico — **Albuquerque**, 1948 western starring Randolph Scott and Barbara Britton

Annapolis, Maryland — **An Annapolis Story**, 1955 romance starring John Derek and Diana Lynn

Aspen, Colorado — **Aspen**, 1977 TV mini-series starring Sam Elliott, Perry King, and Gene Barry

Atlantic City, New Jersey — **Atlantic City**, 1981 drama starring Burt Lancaster and Susan Sarandan

Baltimore, Maryland — **Adventure in Baltimore**, 1949 romance starring Shirley Temple

Big Sur, California — **Celebration at Big Sur**, 1971 rock documentary

Boston, Massachusetts — series of 1940 movies starring Chester Morris as police detective, Boston Blackie — **Meet Boston Blackie, Boston Blackie and the Law, Boston Blackie Booked on Suspicion, Boston Blackie's Chinese Venture**, ...

Chattanooga, Tennessee — **Chattanooga Choo Choo**, 1984 comedy starring Barbara Eden

Cleveland, Ohio — **The Kid from Cleveland**, 1949 drama starring George Brent

Cripple Creek, Colorado — **Cripple Creek**, 1952 western starring George Montgomery

Dallas, Texas — **Dallas**, 1950 western starring Gary Cooper and Ruth Roman; **Debbie Does Dallas**, 1970's x-rated movie

Denver, Colorado — **The Denver and Rio Grande**, 1952 western starring Edmund O'Brien

Detroit, Michigan — **Detroit 9000**, 1973 detective movie starring Alex Rocco and Hari Rhodes; **Inside Detroit**, 1955 drama starring Dennis O'Keefe

Dodge City, Kansas — **Dodge City**, 1939 western Errol Flynn and Olivia de Haviland

Honolulu, Hawaii — **Honolulu**, 1939 musical starring Eleanor Powell and Robert Young

Houston, Texas — **The Houston Story**, 1956 drama starring Gene Barry

Kansas City, Missouri, and Kansas City, Kansas — **Kansas City Confidential**, 1952 drama starring John Payne; **The Kansas City Massacre**, 1975 TV movie drama starring Dale Robertson; **Kansas City Princess**, 1934 comedy starring Joan Blondell and Glenda Farrell

Key Largo, Florida — **Key Largo**, 1948 drama starring Humphrey Bogard and Lauren Bacall

Key West, Florida — **Key West**, 1972 TV movie drama starring Stephen Boyd

Laredo, Texas — **Gunmen from Laredo**, 1959 western starring Robert Knapp and Jana Davi

Lonesome Dove, Texas — **Lonesome Dove**, 1988 TV miniseries starring Robert Duvall and Tommy Lee Jones

Los Angeles, California — **L. A. Bad**, 1985 drama starring Esai Morales, Chuck Bail, Janice Rule

Matewan, West Virginia — **Matewan**, 1987 drama about a coal miner's strike, starring Chris Cooper, Will Oldham, Jace Alexander, and Ken Jenkins

Memphis, Tennessee — **Night Train to Memphis**, 1946 drama starring Roy Acuff

Miami, Florida — **Miami Expose**, 1956 drama starring Lee J. Cobb; **The Miami Story**, 1954 drama starring Barry Sullivan

Milwaukee, Wisconsin — **Two Guys from Milwaukee**, 1946 comedy starring Dennis Morgan and Jack Carson

Monterey, California — **Gun Battle at Monterey**, 1957 western starring Sterling Halden

Nashville, Tennessee — **Nashville**, 1975 comedy starring Henry Gibson and Karen Black; **Nashville Girl**, 1976 drama starring Monica Gayle and Glenn Corbett

New Orleans, Louisiana — **Night in New Orleans**, 1942 drama starring Preston Foster and Patricia Morison; **The Toast of New Orleans**, 1950 romance starring Mario Lanza and Kathryn Grayson

Niagara Falls, New York — **Niagara**, 1953 drama starring Marilyn Monroe and Joseph Cotton

Oklahoma City, Oklahoma — **The Oklahoma City Dolls**, 1981 TV movie starring Susan Blakely and Eddie Albert

Paris, Texas — **Paris, Texas**, 1984 drama starring Harry Dean Stanton and Dean Stockwell

Palm Beach, Florida — **The Palm Beach Story**, 1942 comedy starring Claudette Colbert, Joel McCrea, and Rudy Vallee

Philadelphia, Pennsylvania — **Philadelphia, Here I Come**, 1975 drama starring Donal McCann

Pittsburgh, Pennsylvania — **The Fish That Saved Pittsburgh**, 1980's comedy

Reno, Nevada — **Charlie Chan in Reno**, 1939 mystery starring Sidney Toler

Saint Louis, Missouri — **South of St. Louis**, 1949 western starring Joel McCrea

San Antonio, Texas — **San Antone**, 1953 western starring Rod Cameron; **San Antonio**, 1945 western starring Errol Flynn

San Diego, California — **San Diego, I Love You**, 1944 comedy starring Louise Allbritton, Edward Everett Horton, and Buster Keaton

San Francisco, California — **Incident in San Francisco**, 1970 TV movie starring Richard Kiley; **San Francisco**, 1936 musical romance starring Clark Gable, Jeanette MacDonald, and Spencer Tracy; **San Francisco International Airport**, 1970 TV movie; **The San Francisco Story**, 1952 western starring Joel McCrea

Santa Fe, New Mexico — **Santa Fe**, 1951 western starring Randolph Scott; **Santa Fe Marshall**, 1940 western starring William Boyd, **Santa Fe Passage**, 1955 western starring John Payne

Saratoga Springs, New York — **Saratoga**, 1937 romance starring Clark Gable and Jean Harlow

Skokie, Illinois — **Skokie**, 1981 TV drama starring Danny Kaye

Springfield, Massachusetts — **Springfield Rifles**, 1952 western starring Gary Cooper

Tombstone, Arizona — **Sheriff of Tombstone**, 1941 western starring Roy Rogers and Gabby Hayes; **Train to Tombstone**, 1950 western starring Don Barry and Robert Lowery

Tucson, Arizona — **Gunsmoke in Tucson**, 1958 western starring Mark Stevens and Forrest Tucker; **Tucson**, 1949 western starring Jimmy Lydon and Penny Edwards; **Tucson Raiders**, 1944 western starring Wild Bill Elliott

Tulsa, Oklahoma — **Tulsa**, 1949 drama starring Susan Hayward and Robert Preston; **The Tulsa Kid**, 1940 western starring Don Barry and Noah Beery, Sr.

Virginia City, Nevada — **Virginia City**, 1940 western starring Errol Flynn, Miriam Hopkins, Randolph Scott, and Humphrey Bogart

Waco, Texas — **Waco**, 1966 western starring Howard Keel, Jane Russell, and Brian Donlevy

Washington, D.C. — **Adventure in Washington**, 1941 drama starring Herbert Marshall; **Billy Jack Goes to Washington**, 1977 drama starring Tom Laughlin; **Washington Story**, 1952 drama starring Van Johnson and Patricia Neal

Wichita, Kansas — **Wichita**, 1955 western starring Joel McCrea, Vera Miles, and Lloyd Bridges

Woodstock, New York — **Woodstock**, 1970 rockumentary

Yuma, Arizona — **Yuma**, 1970 TV movie starring Clint Walker and Barry Sullivan

The Road Movies — Starring Bing, Bob, and Dorothy

During the 1940's and 1950's, Bing Crosby, Bob Hope, and Dorothy Lamour starred in a series of romantic comedies about their adventures in foreign lands. Can you complete the titles of the following "road" movies?

1. **The Road to** _____, the first of the road movies (1940). Bob and Bing swear off women until they meet Dorothy Lamour dressed in her famous sarong.
2. **The Road to** _____, 1941 movie with the three stars as circus performers travelling through the jungle looking for a diamond mine.
3. **The Road to** _____, 1942 movie where Bing sells Bob to a slave trader and they both vie for the affections of the princess (Dorothy).
4. **The Road to** _____, 1945 movie about their adventures in the Klondike (with talking animals).
5. **The Road to** _____, 1947 movie with Bob and Bing playing musicians who try to save Dorothy from her evil aunt (Gale Sondergaard).
6. **The Road to** _____, 1952, the only one filmed in color. Bob and Bing save Dorothy from an evil princess and other perils of the jungle.
7. **The Road to** _____, the last of the road movies (1962). Bing and Bob star as con men who get involved with spies and space travel.

1. Singapore   2. Zanzibar   3. Morocco   4. Utopia   5. Rio   6. Bali   7. Hong Kong

The Road to Zanzibar: Bing Crosby and Bob Hope © Paramount Pictures / Shooting Star

Foreign Cities in the Titles of Movies

Movies are not only set in American cities. Indeed, many of the most famous movies are set outside this country. Foreign cities are also featured in the titles of many movies. Can you complete the titles of the following movies by filling in the name of the appropriate foreign city?

1. **An American in _____**, 1941 musical starring Gene Kelly and Leslie Caron
2. **American Werewolf in _____**, 1981 horror movie starring David Naughton and Jenny Agutter
3. **Appointment in _____**, 1943 war movie starring George Sanders and Margueritte Chapman
4. **Blame It on _____**, 1984 drama starring Michael Caine, Joseph Bologna, and Valerie Harper
5. **_____**, the 1942 classic war romance starring Humphrey Bogart, Ingrid Bergman, Peter Lorre
6. **_____ Express**, 1968 TV movie drama starring Gene Barry and John Saxon
7. **_____ Holiday**, 1953 romantic comedy starring Audrey Hepburn and Gregory Peck
8. **Is _____ Burning?**, 1966 war movie starring Charles Boyer and Jean-Paul Belmondo
9. **Last Tango in _____**, 1973 drama starring Marlon Brando and Maria Schneider
10. **_____ on the Hudson**, 1984 comedy starring Robin Williams
11. **The Purple Rose of _____**, 1985 Woody Allen movie starring Mia Farrow and Jeff Daniels
12. **_____ Rose**, 1945 war movie about a famous female propagandist for the Axis powers
13. **The Thief of _____**, 1924, 1940, 1961, and 1978 Arabian Nights romance.

1. Paris (France) 2. London (England) 3. Berlin (Germany) 4. Rio (Rio de Janeiro, Brazil) 5. Casablanca (Morocco) 6. Istanbul (Turkey)
7. Roman (Rome, Italy) 8. Paris (France) 9. Paris (France) 10. Moscow (Russia) 11. Cairo, Egypt 12. Tokyo (Japan) 13. Baghdad (Iraq)

Made-for-TV Movies

1. TV movies, like most movies, tend to be located in New York, Los Angeles, overseas, or in some anonymous setting. In the 1970's, however, Boston was a popular setting for TV movies. Can you name two recent TV movies located in Boston?

2. The 1970's true-life drama, **Brian's Song**, depicted the friendship between two professional football players, Gale Sayers (Billy Dee Williams) and Brian Piccolo (James Caan), as Brian fought a losing battle against cancer. What team did they play for?

3. **Friendly Fire**, a 1979 drama, starred Carol Burnett and Ned Beatty as two midwestern parents trying to find out the truth about the death of their son in Vietnam, where he was killed by friendly fire from American artillery. Where were they from?

4. Ned Beatty, along with Kurt Russell, also starred in the 1975 TV movie, **The Deadly Tower**, which dramatized the true story of Charles Whitman, a mass killer who shot 13 people and wounded another 34 from his vantage point on top of a university tower. Where did this massacre occur?

5. **Mary White** was a 1977 TV movie biography which told the story of the relationship between William Allen White (Ed Flanders), the famous journalist, and his daughter, Mary (Kathleen Beller) — and how he survived her death at the age of sixteen (from an accident while horseback riding). William Allen White was the editor of what small midwestern paper.

1. The Last Hurrah, Miles to Go Before I Sleep, See How She Runs, Two on a Bench 2. Chicago (Illinois) Bears 3. La Porte City, Iowa 4. Austin, Texas 5. Emporia (Kansas) Gazette

More Made-for-TV Movies

Can you match the following TV movies with the towns in which they were set? [Expert rating: 8 out of 13]

1. **Birds of Prey**, 1973 thriller starring David Janssen and Ralph Meeker
2. **The City**, 1971 drama starring Anthony Quinn and E. G. Marshall
3. **Code Name: Diamond Head**, 1977 starring Roy Thinnes and France Nuyen
4. **Crawlspace**, 1972 drama starring Arthur Kennedy and Teresa Wright
5. **The Day After**, 1986 drama about a nuclear strike
6. **The Deadly Triangle**, 1977 starring Dale Robinette and Taylor Lacher
7. **The Defection of Simas Kudirka**, 1978 drama starring Alan Arkin
8. **Dr. Max**, 1974 drama starring Lee J. Cobb and Janet Ward
9. **F Scott Fitzgerald & the Cast of Belles**, 1974 biography starring Richard Chamberlain and Blythe Danner
10. **A Fire in the Sky**, 1978 drama starring Richard Crenna, Elizabeth Ashley
11. **The Gambler, Part III**, 1988 western starring Kenny Rogers
12. **The Girls in the Office**, 1979 starring Susan Saint James and Barbara Eden
13. **Guilty or Innocent**, 1975 biography of Dr. Sam Sheppard (George Peppard)

a. Albuquerque, New Mexico
b. Baltimore, Maryland
c. Bismarck, North Dakota
d. Cleveland, Ohio
e. Honolulu, Hawaii
f. Houston, Texas
g. Lawrence, Kansas
h. Montgomery, Alabama
i. Norwalk, Connecticut
j. Phoenix, Arizona
k. Portsmouth, New Hampshire
l. Salt Lake City, Utah
m. Sun Valley, Idaho

Answers: 1. l 2. a 3. e 4. i 5. g 6. m 7. k 8. b 9. h 10. j 11. c 12. f 13. d

Even More Made-for-TV Movies

Can you match the following TV movies with the towns in which they were set? [Expert rating: 8 out of 13]

1. **Lady of the House**, 1978 biography of Sally Stanford starring Dyan Cannon
2. **The Last Day**, 1975 western starring Richard Widmark and Robert Conrad
3. **The Legend of Lizzie Borden**, 1975 drama starring Elizabeth Montgomery
4. **Long Gone**, 1986 drama
5. **Longarm**, 1988 pilot for a western series
6. **Murder at the World Series**, 1977 thriller starring Linda Day George
7. **Murder in Music City**, 1979 starring Sonny Bono and Lee Purcell
8. **The Murder of Mary Phagen**, 1988 true-life drama starring Jack Lemmon
9. **Ransom for Alice!**, 1977 western starring Gil Gerard and Yvette Mimieux
10. **Ruby and Oswald**, 1978 bio starring Michael Lerner and Frederic Forrest
11. **The Silence**, 1975 drama starring Richard Thomas and Cliff Gorman
12. **Vanishing Act**, 1986 mystery starring Mike Farrell and Elliott Gould
13. **When Every Day Was the Fourth of July**, 1978 drama starring Dean Jones

a. Atlanta, Georgia
b. Banff, Alberta
c. Bridgeport, Connecticut
d. Coffeyville, Kansas
e. Dallas, Texas
f. Fall River, Massachusetts
g. Houston, Texas
h. Nashville, Tennessee
i. Santa Fe, New Mexico
j. Sausalito, California
k. Seattle, Washington
l. Tampico, Illinois
m. West Point, New York

Answers: 1. j 2. d 3. f 4. l 5. i 6. g 7. h 8. a 9. k 10. e 11. m 12. b 13. c

73

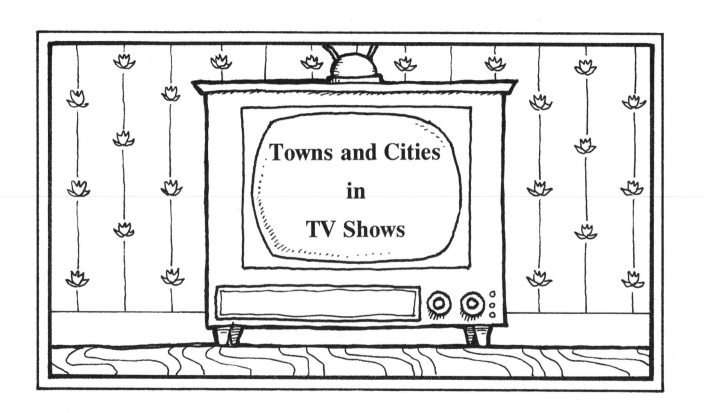

Towns and Cities

in

TV Shows

Turning on Your Television

This second section of **Tinseltowns, U.S.A.** features over 400 television shows, both old and new, which have been set in a specific town or city. The television shows are as varied as the movies in the previous section, including everything from westerns and detective shows to situation comedies and variety shows.

Don't be surprised if you don't recognize all the shows listed here, because some of them had very short lives (one or two episodes) before they were sent off to *The Twilight Zone*, or to Ork, or to whatever graveyard such shows are sent.

Anyway, the following pages should bring back "the thrilling days of yesteryear" for you.

As with the movies, if you know of any other television shows where a town or city is featured prominently as part of the show, please send me the information. Again, I'll include any new contributions in future editions of this book. If you send me something I don't already have, I'll send you an autographed copy of the latest edition and will also list your name in the preface of the book. Send information to me at the following address: **John Kremer, c/o Ad-Lib Publications, 51 N. Fifth Street, Fairfield, IA 52556-3226**.

Thanks for your help.

Television Firsts

1. What station broadcast the first TV show in 1928?

2. Where was the first educational TV station (1933)?

3. KC2XAK was the first UHF TV station in 1949. Where was it located?

4. KPTV was the first commercial UHF TV station in 1952. Where was it located?

5. Where did the first televised wedding take place?

6. Where is the first cable TV station run entirely by 9 to 14-year-olds?

7. Where was the first color TV studio in the United States?

8. What was the first town to star in a beer commercial (for Miller Lite)?

9. What was the first town to be named after a TV game show?

1. WRBG-TV of Schenectady, New York 2. University of Iowa in Iowa City, Iowa 3. Bridgeport, Connecticut 4. Portland, Oregon 5. Des Plaines, Illinois 6. KIDS-TV in Sun Prairie, Wisconsin 7. NBC studios in Burbank, California 8. Barneveld, Wisconsin 9. In March 1950, the citizens of Hot Springs, New Mexico, change the name of their town to Truth or Consequences, New Mexico

Television Network Headquarters

While most major TV networks have their headquarters in New York (including ABC, CBS, NBC, ESPN, MTV, HBO, A&E, USA, and Lifetime), the growth of cable TV and independent stations has resulted in many new networks starting up in other areas of the country. Can you name the headquarter cities of the following networks? Match each network with the appropriate city (the answers are at the bottom of the next page). [Expert rating: 8 out of 14]

1. Alaska Television Network
2. Cable News Network
3. Canadian Broadcasting System
4. CTV (Canadian TV)
5. The Disney Channel
6. Fox Broadcasting System
7. Hispanic/American Broadcasting Company
8. Home Shopping Network
9. Montana Television Network
10. Mutual Broadcasting Network
11. The Nashville Network
12. Public Broadcasting System
13. RFD-TV
14. You TV Cable Network

a. Anchorage, Alaska
b. Arlington, Virginia
c. Atlanta, Georgia
d. Billings, Montana
e. Burbank, California
f. Clearwater, Florida
g. Hialeah, Florida
h. Los Angeles, Califorina
i. Nashville, Tennessee
j. Omaha, Nebraska
k. Ottawa, Ontario
l. Pittsburgh, Pennsylvania
m. Toronto, Ontario
n. Washington, D.C.

Religious Broadcasting Networks

There are almost as many religious broadcasting networks as secular. Can you name the home bases of the following religious broadcasting networks. Match the network with the town or city in which it is based. [Expert rating: 4 out of 8]

1. American Christian Television System (ACTS)
2. Christian Broadcasting Network (CBN)
3. Christian Television Network (CTN)
4. Eternal Word Television Network
5. National Christian Network (NCN)
6. National Jewish Television
7. Praise the Lord Network (PTL)
8. Trinity Broadcasting Network (TBN)

a. Birmingham, Alabama
b. Clearwater, Florida
c. Cocoa, Florida
d. Fort Mill, South Carolina
e. Fort Worth, Texas
f. Riverdale, New York
g. Santa Ana, California
h. Virginia Beach, Virginia

TV Shows of the 1950's — Comedies

Many television shows are set in specific towns or cities. Can you name where the following late 40's and 1950's comedy shows were located?

1. **Bachelor Father**, starring John Forsythe and Noreen Corcoran
2. **The Brothers**, starring Gale Gordon, Bob Sweeney, and Ann Morriss
3. **The Charlie Farrell Show**, starring Charlie Farrell and Charles Winninger
4. **A Date with Judy**, starring Mary Linn Beller and John Gibson
5. **Hennesey**, drama starring Jackie Cooper, Abby Dalton, Arte Johnson
6. **Lum & Abner Show**, starring Chester Lauck and Norris Goff
7. **Mama**, starring Peggy Wood and Judson Laire
8. **Mr. Peepers**, starring Wally Cox
9. **Norby**, starring David Wayne and Joan Lorring
10. **The Peter & Mary Show**, starring Peter Lind Hayes and Mary Healy
11. **The Ray Bolger Show**, starring Ray Bolger, Allyn Joslyn, Betty Lynn

a. Beverly Hills, California
b. Jefferson, Missouri
c. New Rochelle, New York
d. Palm Springs, California
e. Pearl River, New York
f. Pelham, New York
g. Pine Ridge, Arkansas
h. San Diego, California
i. San Francisco, California
j. San Francisco, California
k. Santa Barbara, California

Answers: 1. a   2. i / j   3. d   4. k   5. h   6. g   7. i / j   8. b   9. e   10. c   11. f

Other TV Shows of the 1950's

Can you match the following 1950's shows with their locations? [Expert rating: 8 out of 11]

1. **The Alaskans,** adventure starring Roger Moore and Jeff York

2. **Bourbon Street Beat,** detective starring Andrew Duggan, Richard Long

3. **Casey Jones,** 1957 historical drama

4. **Grand Ole Opry,** 1955-1956 musical variety show

5. **Hayloft Hoedown,** 1948 musical variety show

6. **M Squad,** police drama starring Lee Marvin and Paul Newlan

7. **Manhunt,** police drama starring Victor Jory and Patrick McVey

8. **Ozark Jubilee,** 1955-1960 musical variety show

9. **Pete Kelly's Blues,** police drama starring William Reynolds

10. **The Sheriff of Cochise,** police drama starring John Bromfield, Stan Jones

11. **The Wonderful John Acton,** drama starring Harry Holcombe

a. Bisbee, Arizona

b. Chicago, Illinois

c. Jackson, Tennessee

d. Kansas City, Missouri

e. Ludlow, Kentucky

f. Nashville, Tennessee

g. New Orleans, Louisiana

h. Philadelphia, Pennsylvania

i. San Diego, California

j. Skagway, Alaska

k. Springfield, Missouri

Answers: 1. j   2. g   3. c   4. f   5. h   6. b   7. i   8. k   9. d   10. a   11. e

TV Locations — Crime and Punishment

Why are most police and detective shows located in New York City or Los Angeles? Is it because these cities have the highest crime rates? Or the best detectives? Or is it because they are the easiest cities to film? Whatever the reason, these two cities are certainly the most popular with TV writers and producers.

1. Name five police or detective shows located in the Los Angeles, California area.

2. Name five police or detective shows located in New York, New York.

3. Probably the most popular crime city after New York and Los Angeles is San Francisco, California. Name five police or detective shows set in San Francisco.

4. Name three set in Chicago, Illinois.

5. Name three set in Boston, Massachusetts.

6. Name three set in San Diego, California.

7. Name three set in Honolulu, Hawaii.

8. Name three detective or spy shows set in Washington, DC.

1. The following police and detective shows have been set in Los Angeles, California — Adam 12; Arrest and Trial; Banyon; Baretta; Barnaby Jones; Beverly Hills Buntz; The Blue Knight; Blue Thunder; Burke's Law; Cannon; Charlie's Angels; Chase; CHIPS; Columbo; The Cop & the Kid; The D.A.; Dan Raven; Delvecchio; Dragnet; The Devlin Connection; Emergency; Fall Guy; Faraday & Company; Get Christie Love; The Greatest American Hero; Griff; Hardcastle & McCormick; Hart to Hart; Honey West; Hunter; Kate Loves a Mystery; Knight Rider; Mannix; Markham; McClain's Law; Men at Law; The Mod Squad; Moonlighting; The Most Deadly Game; Ohara; The Outsider; The Partners; Perry Mason; Police Story; Police Woman; Private Eye; Quincy, M.E.; Remington Steele; Richie Brockelman, Private Eye; Riker; Riptide; The Rockford Files; 77 Sunset Strip; The Smith Family; Starsky & Hutch; The Storefront Lawyers; Strike Force; Switch; T. J. Hooker; Tenafly; Tenspeed and Brown Shoe; 240 Roberts; Waterfront; Whiz Kids

Here are some others set in southern California — The A-Team; The Bionic Woman; Bronk; Chopper One; Dan August; Felony Squad; Harbor Command; Jake and the Fatman; Jessie; Kate McShane; Knight Rider; Matt Helm; The Protectors; The Rookies; The Six-Million Dollar Man; S.W.A.T.

2. Among the shows set in New York are the following — The Asphalt Jungle; Barney Blake, Police Reporter; Barney Miller; Brenner; Cagney & Lacey; Car 54, Where Are You?; The Cases of Eddie Drake; Charlie Wild, Private Detective; City Detective; Coronet Blue; Craig Kennedy, Criminologist; Crime Photographer; Crime with Father; The D.A.'s Man; Decoy; The Defenders; Detective School; The Detective's Wife; Diagnosis: Unknown; Dick Tracy; 87th Precinct; Eischied; Ellery Queen; The Equalizer; The Files of Jeffrey Jones; For the People; Front Page Detective; Harrigan & Son; Hawk; I Cover Times Square; I'm the Law; The Investigator; The Investigators; Jimmy Hughes, Rookie Cop; Johnny Midnight; Johnny Staccato; Justice; Kojak; The Lawless Years; Madigan; Manimal; The Mask; McCloud; Mickey Spillane's Mike Hammer; Mr. and Mrs. Mystery; N.Y.P.D.; Naked City; New York Confidential; The Plainclothesman; Police Story; Richard Diamond, Private Detective; Rocky King, Detective; Shaft; The Snoop Sisters; Spiderman; The Telltale Club; The Thin Man; The Trials of O'Brien; The Walter Winchell File

3. These shows were set in San Francisco — Amy Prentiss; Bert D'Angelo, Superstar; Checkmate; Foul Play; Freebie and the Bean; Hagen; Hooperman; Ironside; Khan!; Kingston Confidential; McMillan & Wife; Mysteries of Chinatown; Partners in Crime; Racket Squad; Sam Benedict; The Streets of San Francisco

4. Chicago crime shows — Chicago Story; Crime Story; The Duke; Lady Blue; They Stand Accused; The Untouchables

5. Boston detective shows — Banacek; Boston Blackie; The Law and Harry McGraw; Spenser: For Hire; The Young Lawyers

6. San Diego detective shows — Coronado 9; Harry O, Manhunt; Simon and Simon

7. Honolulu police shows — Hawaii Five-O; Hawaiian Eye; Hawaiian Heat; Jake and the Fatman (starting in 1989); Magnum, P.I.

8. Washington, D.C. spy and police shows — Adderly; The F.B.I.; Get Smart; Scarecrow and Mrs. King; Wonder Woman

TV Detective Shows of the 1960's

Can you name the locations of the following 1960's TV police and detective shows? [Expert rating: 4 out of 6]

1. **Dante**, 1960-1961 mystery adventure starring Howard Duff, Alan Mowbray, and James Nolan

2. **Hawaiian Eye**, 1959-1963 detective starring Bob Conrad, Connie Stevens, and Troy Donahue

3. **Judd, For the Defense**, 1967-1969 drama starring Carl Betz and Stephen Young

4. **Michael Shayne, Private Detective**, 1960-1961 detective starring Richard Denning and Jerry Paris

5. **Surfside Six**, 1960-1962 detective starring Van Williams and Lee Patterson

6. **The Untouchables**, 1959-1963 police drama starring Robert Stack and Abel Fernandez

To help you out, here are the choices: Chicago, Honolulu, Houston, Miami, Miami Beach, and San Francisco

1. San Francisco, California   2. Honolulu, Hawaii   3. Houston, Texas   4. Miami Beach, Florida   5. Miami, Florida   6. Chicago, Illinois

Westerns — The Good Guys and the Bad Buys

During the late 1950's and early 1960's western dramas dominated the TV landscape. It was possible at one time to watch a western almost any hour of any day during prime time. It was heaven on earth for a growing boy like me. Can you match the following 1950's western shows with the towns in which they were located? [Expert rating: 6 out of 8]

1. **The Adventures of Jim Bowie**, starring Scott Forbes
2. **Broken Arrow**, starring John Lupton and Michael Ansara
3. **The Californians**, starring Adam Kennedy, and Richard Coogan
4. **Hotel de Paree**, starring Earl Holliman and Judi Meredith
5. **Law of the Plainsman**, starring Michael Ansara and Dayton Lummis
6. **The Lawman**, starring John Russell, Peter Brown, Bek Nelson
7. **Yancy Derringer**, starring Jock Mahoney, X Brands, Julie Adams
8. **Zorro**, starring Guy Williams and Gene Sheldon

a. Georgetown, Colorado
b. Laramie, Wyoming
c. Monterey, California
d. New Orleans, Louisiana
e. New Orleans, Louisiana
f. San Francisco, California
g. Santa Fe, New Mexico
h. Tucson, Arizona

Answers: 1. d / e   2. h   3. f   4. a   5. g   6. b   7. d / e   8. c

Westerns in the 1960's

Can you match these popular 1960's westerns to the towns they were located in? [Expert rating: 11 out of 13]

1. **The Big Valley**, starring Barbara Stanwyck, Richard Long, Lee Majors
2. **Bonanza**, starring Lorne Green, Michael Landon, and Dan Blocker
3. **The Dakotas**, starring Larry Ward, Jack Elam, and Chad Everett
4. **Dundee and the Culcane**, starring John Mills and Sean Garrison
5. **Gunsmoke**, starring James Arness, Amanda Blake, and Milburn Stone
6. **Have Gun, Will Travel**, starring Richard Boone
7. **High Chaparral**, starring Leif Erickson and Cameron Mitchell
8. **Klondike**, starring Ralph Teager and James Coburn
9. **The Legend of Jesse James**, starring Christopher Jones and Allen Case
10. **The Outlaws**, starring Barton MacLane, Don Collier, and Slim Pickens
11. **The Road West**, starring Barry Sullivan and Andrew Prine
12. **The Virginian**, starring James Drury, Lee J. Cobb, and Doug McClure
13. **Whispering Smith**, starring Audie Murphy and Guy Mitchell

a. Denver, Colorado
b. Dodge City, Kansas
c. Lawrence, Kansas
d. Medicine Bow, Wyoming
e. Rapid City, South Dakota
f. Saint Joseph, Missouri
g. San Francisco, California
h. Sausalito, California
i. Skagway, Alaska
j. Stillwater, Oklahoma
k. Stockton, California
l. Tucson, Arizona
m. Virginia City, Nevada

Answers: 1. k   2. m   3. e   4. h   5. b   6. g   7. l   8. i   9. f   10. j   11. c   12. d   13. a

Bonanza: Dan Blocker, Lorne Green, Michael Landon

TV Shows of the 1960's

1. One of my favorite shows of the late 1960's was **Rowan and Martin's Laugh-In**, starring Dan Rowan, Dick Martin, and an assortment of wonderfully zany characters. Do you remember the location for this comedy variety show? [Hint: It was located in "beautiful downtown _____".]

2. My favorite cartoon of the 1960's was the **Rocky and Bullwinkle Show**, starring Rocky the Squirrel and Bullwinkle the Moose as well as their nemeses, Boris Badenov and Natasha Fatale. What northern town was home base for Rocky and Bullwinkle?

3. After the success of the **Batman** show in 1966 (set in the fictitious Gotham City), two takeoffs of other comicbook heroes appeared, **T.H.E. Cat** starring Robert Loggia and **The Green Hornet** starring Van Williams and Bruce Lee. What cities served as home bases for these two heroes?

4. **Follow the Sun** was a short-lived adventure series about two freelance magazine writers (Barry Coe and Brett Halsey). Where was it set?

5. Gary Lockwood, who had a subsidiary role in **Follow the Sun**, later starred in his own short-lived drama about a newly-commissioned officer in the Marine Corps (Robert Vaughn played his captain). **The Lieutenant** was stationed at what Marine Corp base?

6. After the great success of ABC's prime-time soap opera, **Peyton Place**, CBS tried out a spinoff of its own successful daytime soap, **As the World Turns**. This spinoff, **Our Private World**, featured Eileen Fulton as Lisa Hughes, a young divorcee in Chicago, and Geraldine Fitzgerald as the matriarch of an extremely wealthy family, the Eldridges. In what exclusive suburb did the Eldridges live?

7. Most of the daytime soap operas are situated in fictitious communities. **Days of Our Lives** (starring Mary Beth Evans and Stephen Nichols, among others), however, is set in a New England town. What is the name of that town?

8. Another daytime soap opera, **One Life to Live** (starring Erika Slezak and Clint Ritchie), is located in what large eastern city?

9. One of the most popular shows of the late 1960's and early 1970's was **Marcus Welby, M.D.,** a medical drama starring Robert Young and James Brolin. Where was his practice located?

1. beautiful downtown Burbank   2. International Falls, Minnesota (sometimes known as Frostbite Falls, Minnesota)   3. The Cat: San Francisco, California, and The Green Hornet: Washington, D.C.   4. Honolulu, Hawaii   5. Camp Pendleton in Oceanside, California   6. Lake Forest, Illinois 7. Salem, Massachusetts   8. Philadelphia, Pennsylvania   9. Santa Monica, California

Television Series on the Move

Television series don't always stay in one place. Characters sometime move on to bigger and better, or just plain different, places.

1. Harry Orwell (David Janssen), the detective in the 1970's series, **Harry-O**, moved between seasons. What city did he move from, and what city did he move to?

2. **My Three Sons**, the 1960's comedy starring Fred MacMurray, was first located in the fictional town of Bryant Park, somewhere in the midwest. In 1967 the family moved to a new city. What was the name of that real-life city?

3. Hugh O'Brien was sheriff of three different towns during his six seasons starring as Wyatt Earp in the 1950's western, **The Life and Legend of Wyatt Earp**. What were the names of the three towns?

4. **American Bandstand**, the perennial rock'n'roll show hosted by Dick Clark, started in what city? Where is it now located?

5. The various incarnations of **I Love Lucy** and **The Lucy Show**, starring Lucille Ball, were located in at least six different cities? Name at least three of them.

6. The 1960's western **Rawhide**, starring Clint Eastwood, told the story of cattle drivers taking herds between what two western towns?

7. The recent series, **Crime Story**, first featured 1950's cops in what city? The second season, these same cops moved to another city. What city did they move to?

8. The **Donny and Marie** (Osmond) show was first produced in Hollywood, California. Later the show was moved back to their hometown where the Osmond family built their own studio. Where is their hometown?

9. In **The Travels of Jaimie McPheeters**, a 1963-1964 western starring Kurt Russell, passed through what towns?

10. Sally Jesse Raphael, the host of her own talk show, started out in what midwestern city? From what city does her show now originate?

11. From 1967 to 1974, Phil Donahue hosted the **Donahue** talk show in what city? From 1974 through 1985 his show originate from what city? And, finally, from what city does his show now originate?

1. San Diego, California, to Santa Monica, California 2. North Hollywood, California 3. Ellsworth, Kansas; Dodge City, Kansas; and Tombstone, Arizona 4. Philadelphia, Pennsylvania; Los Angeles, California 5. 623 East 68th Street #4A, New York, New York (1950-1954); Hollywood, California (1954-1955); Westport, Connecticut (1957 and 1960); Danfield, Connecticut (1961-1965); San Francisco, California (1965-1968); Los Angeles, California (1968-1974) 6. San Antonio, Texas, and Sedalia, Kansas 7. Chicago, Illinois; Las Vegas, Nevada 8. Orem, Utah 9. Paducah, Kentucky - Saint Louis, Missouri - Fort Bridger, Wyoming - Salt Lake City, Utah - Sacramento, California 10. Saint Louis, Missouri; New Haven, Connecticut 11. Dayton, Ohio; Chicago, Illinois; New York, New York

TV Comedies of the 1960's

While many of the situation comedies of the 1960's were located in some anonymous or fictitious midwestern city, a number of them were set in actual cities other than New York or Los Angeles. Can you match the following 1960's comedies with their setting? [Expert rating: 9 out of 13]

1. **Bewitched**, starring Elizabeth Montgomery and Dick York

2. **The Dick Van Dyke Show**, starring Dick Van Dyke and Mary Tyler Moore

3. **The Doris Day Show**, starring Doris Day, Denver Pyle, and Rose Marie

4. **The Farmer's Daughter**, starring Inger Stevens and William Windom

5. **The Flying Nun**, starring Sally Field

6. **Gidget**, starring Sally Field, Don Porter, and Betty Conner

7. **Glynis**, starring Glynis Johns and Keith Andes

8. **Happy**, starring David and Steven Born and Yvonne Lime

9. **Here Comes the Brides**, starring Bobby Sherman and David Soul

10. **I Dream of Jeannie**, starring Barbara Eden, Larry Hagman, and Bill Daily

11. **Love on a Rooftop**, starring Peter Deuel, Judy Carne, and Rich Little

12. **Mickey**, starring Mickey Rooney

13. **The Tab Hunter Show**, starring Tab Hunter

a. Cocoa Beach, Florida
b. Malibu, California
c. Mill Valley, California
d. New Rochelle, New York
e. Newport Beach, California
f. Palm Springs, California
g. San Diego, California
h. San Francisco, California
i. San Juan, Puerto Rico
j. Santa Monica, California
k. Seattle, Washington
l. Washington, D. C.
m. Westport, Connecticut

Answers: 1. m   2. d   3. c   4. l   5. i   6. j   7. g   8. f   9. k   10. a   11. h   12. e   13. b

1970's TV Police and Detective Shows

    While many police and detective shows are located in New York or Los Angeles, some are located in other regions of the country. Can you name the locals of the following 1970's TV detective shows? [Expert rating: 6 out of 8]

1. **Banacek**, starring George Peppard

2. **Big Shamus, Little Shamus**, starring Brian Dennehy and Doug McKeon

3. **Hart to Hart**, starring Robert Wagner and Stephanie Powers

4. **Hawaii Five-O**, starring Jack Lord, James MacArthur, and Kam Fong

5. **Kolchak: The Night Stalker**, starring Darren McGavin

6. **Longstreet**, starring James Franciscus and Marlyn Mason

7. **Nakia**, starring Robert Forster and Arthur Kennedy

8. **Toma**, starring Tony Musante and Simon Oakland

a. Albuquerque, New Mexico

b. Atlantic City, New Jersey

c. Beverly Hills, California

d. Boston, Massachusetts

e. Chicago, Illinois

f. Honolulu, Hawaii

g. New Orleans, Louisiana

h. Newark, New Jersey

Answers: 1. d   2. b   3. c   4. f   5. e   6. g   7. a   8. h

Television Shows of the 1970's

1. **The Bionic Woman**, starring Lindsay Wagner, operated out of southern California. Where was her home located?

2. **The Young Rebels** (starring Rick Ely, Louis Gossett Jr., Alex Henteloff, and Hilary Thompson) was a fall 1970 adventure series that told the story of four young protestors during the American Revolution. The young rebels operated out of what small Pennsylvania city?

3. The 1970's was not a big decade for westerns. Indeed, few new westerns survived more than one season. Can you name the location of the 1975-1976 western, **The Barbary Coast**, starring Doug McClure and William Shatner?

4. In the spring of 1979, NBC experimented with a new series concept, the cliff hanger. The show, **Cliff Hangers**, was made up of three 20-minute segments that continued from one week to the next with the hero or heroine always left in a perilous situation at the end of each show. Can you name the locations of the three segments that were part of **Cliff Hangers**?

    a. **The Curse of Dracula**, an occult thriller starring Michael Nouri as the evil Count.

    b. **The Secret Empire**, part western and part science fiction; starring Geoffrey Scott.

    c. **Stop Susan Williams**, a newspaper thriller starring Susan Anton.

Just in case you didn't know, the experiment failed. In fact, only one of the three segments ran its full length. The other two left not only the hero or heroine hanging but also the audience.

5. Before **Dallas** and **Dynasty**, there were the soap operas, **Peyton Place** and **Family**. **Family** told the story of a middle-class family in what California city?

6. Even before **Family**, there was the historical soap opera **Beacon Hill**, starring Roy Cooper, David Dukes, and Nancy Marchand. In which city was it situated?

7. In 1976, Jim Bouton, a former big-league baseball pitcher, starred in a short-lived comedy named after his best-selling book, **Ball Four**. In the TV series, what team did he play for?

8. The Second City comedy group started out in Chicago, America's second city. When, however, the Second City group came to TV as **Second City TV**, the show featured comedians from an offshoot of the original troupe (including Joe Flaherty, Andrea Martin, Harold Ramis, John Candy, Rick Moranis, and Eugene Levy). From what city did the TV show originate?

9. **Wheels** was a 1970 miniseries, starring Rock Hudson and Lee Remick, based on Arthur Hailey's best-selling novel of the same name. What industry did it feature? In what city?

1. Ojai, California   2. Chester, Pennsylvania   3. San Francisco, California [Be honest now, did you know the answer because you saw the series or because you knew where the Barbary Coast is located?]   4. a. San Francisco, California   b. Cheyenne, Wyoming   c. Washington, D.C.   5. Pasadena, California   6. Boston, Massachusetts   7. the Washington, D.C. Nationals   8. Toronto, Ontario   9. the automotive industry; Detroit, Michigan

TV Comedy Shows of the 1970's

During the 1970's, situation comedies went regional. While most previous comedies were located in New York, Los Angeles, or some anonymous town, the 1970's comedies took pride in showcasing the cities in which they were supposed to be located.

1. Can you name the two hit comedies which were located in Milwaukee, Wisconsin?

2. Can you name three 1970's comedies set in Chicago, Illinois?

3. Can you name three set in Washington, D.C.?

4. Can you name two set in San Francisco, California?

5. Scott Baio, Caren Kaye, and Lynda Goodfriend starred in two short-lived comedies about Las Vegas show girls with children. Can you name the two shows?

1. Happy Days; Laverne and Shirley   2. Bob Newhart Show; The Chicago Teddy Bears; Good Times; Out of the Blue; Working Stiffs   3. All's Fair; Ball Four; Grandpa Goes to Washington; Karen; Szysznyk; Temperature Rising; That's My Mama   4. The Doris Day Show; House Calls; Phyllis   5. Blansky's Beauties (also starring Nancy Walker and Pat Morita) and Who's Watching the Kids?

The Mary Tyler Moore Show: Mary, Georgia, and Ted   © Yoram Kamana / Shooting Star

More 1970's Situation Comedies

Can you match the following situation comedies with their cities? [Expert rating: 10 out of 12]

1. **Alice**, starring Linda Lavin, Vic Tayback, and Beth Howland
2. **Angie**, starring Donna Pescow and Robert Hays
3. **Apple Pie**, starring Rue McClanahan and Dabney Coleman
4. **CPO Sharkey**, starring Don Rickles, Peter Isacksen, and Jeff Hollis
5. **The Don Rickles Show**, starring Don Rickles, Louise Sorel, Erin Moran
6. **The Facts of Life**, starring Charlotte Rae, Lisa Whelchel, Nancy McKeon
7. **Hee Haw Honeys**, starring Kathie Lee Johnson, Misty Rowe, Lulu Roman
8. **Hello, Larry**, starring McLean Stevenson and Kim Richards
9. **Joe and Sons**, starring Richard Castellano and Jerry Stiller
10. **Joe's World**, starring Ramon Bieri, K Callan, and Melissa Sherman
11. **The Mary Tyler Moore Show**, starring Mary Tyler Moore, Edward Asner
12. **Maude**, starring Beatrice Arthur and Bill Macy

a. Detroit, Michigan
b. Great Neck, New York
c. Hoboken, New Jersey
d. Kansas City, Missouri
e. Minneapolis, Minnesota
f. Nashville, Tennessee
g. Peekskill, New York
h. Philadelphia, Pennsylvania
i. Phoenix, Arizona
j. Portland, Oregon
k. San Diego, California
l. Tuckhoe, New York

Answers: 1. i   2. h   3. d   4. k   5. b   6. g   7. f   8. j   9. c   10. a   11. e   12. l   13. b

Even More 1970's Situation Comedies

Can you match the following situation comedies with their cities? [Expert rating: 10 out of 12]

1. **The McLean Stevenson Show**, starring McLean Stevenson
2. **The Montefuscos**, starring Joe Sirola, Naomi Stevens, and Ron Carey
3. **Mork & Mindy**, starring Robin Williams and Pam Dawber
4. **The New Dick Van Dyke Show**, starring Dick Van Dyke and Hope Lange
5. **One Day at a Time**, starring Bonnie Franklin and Mackenzie Phillips
6. **The Roller Girls**, starring Terry Kiser and Rhonda Bates
7. **Shirley**, starring Shirley Jones and Patrick Wayne
8. **Sunshine**, starring Cliff DeYoung and Elizabeth Cheshire
9. **Three's Company**, starring John Ritter, Joyce DeWitt, Suzanne Sommers
10. **The Tony Randall Show**, starring Tony Randall and Barney Martin
11. **A Touch of Grace**, starring Shirley Booth and J. Patrick O'Malley
12. **WKRP**, starring Gary Sandy, Gordon Jump, and Loni Anderson

a. Boulder, Colorado
b. Cincinnati, Ohio
c. Evanston, Illinois
d. Indianapolis, Indiana
e. New Canaan, Connecticut
f. Oakland, California
g. Philadelphia, Pennsylvania
h. Phoenix, Arizona
i. Pittsburgh, Pennsylvania
j. Santa Monica, California
k. Tahoe City, California
l. Vancouver, British Columbia

Answers: 1. c   2. e   3. a   4. h   5. d   6. i   7. k   8. l   9. j   10. g   11. f   12. b

Drama in the 1970's

Can you name the locations of the following 1970's TV dramas? [Expert rating: 12 out of 18]

1. **Eight Is Enough**, starring Dick Van Patten, Adam Rich, Betty Buckley
2. **The Fitzpatricks**, starring Bert Kramer and Mariclare Costello
3. **From Here to Eternity**, starring William Devane and Natalie Wood
4. **The Innocent and the Damned**, starring Sam Elliott, Perry King, Gene Barry
5. **James at 15**, starring Lance Kerwin, Linden Chiles, Lynn Carlin
6. **Little House on the Prairie**, starring Michael Landon and Karen Grassle
7. **Lou Grant**, starring Edward Asner, Mason Adams, Linda Kelsey
8. **Lucas Tanner** , starring David Hartman and Rosemary Murphy
9. **The Man and the City**, starring Anthony Quinn, Mike Farrell, Mala Powers
10. **Owen Marshall, Counselor at Law**, starring Arthur Hill and Lee Majors
11. **The Paper Chase**, starring John Houseman and James Stephens
12. **Police Surgeon**, starring Sam Groom and Jack Albertson
13. **Sarge**, starring George Kennedy and Sallie Shockley
14. **The Senator**, starring Hal Holbrook and Michael Tolan
15. **Sons and Daughters**, starring Gary Frank and Glynnis O'Connor
16. **Studs Lonigan**, starring Harry Hamlin and Colleen Dewhurst
17. **Trapper John, M.D.**, starring Pernell Roberts and Gregory Harrison
18. **The Waltons**, starring Ralph Waite, Michael Learned, Richard Thomas

a. Albuquerque, New Mexico
b. Aspen, Colorado
c. Boston, Massachusetts
d. Cambridge, Massachusetts
e. Chicago, Illinois
f. Flint, Michigan
g. Honolulu, Hawaii
h. Los Angeles, California
i. Sacramento, California
j. San Diego, California
k. San Francisco, California
l. Santa Barbara, California
m. Stockton, California
n. Toronto, Ontario
o. Walnut Grove, Minnesota
p. Walton's Mountain, Virginia
q. Washington, D.C.
r. Webster Groves, Missouri

Answers: 1. i 2. f 3. g 4. b 5. c 6. o 7. h 8. r 9. a 10. l 11. d 12. n 13. j 14. q 15. m 16. e 17. k 18. p

Religious Shows on Television

With the PTL and Jimmy Swaggart scandals, religious broadcasters have been very much in the news. Can you name the home bases of the following religious shows? Match the show to the city from which it originates. [Expert rating: 8 out of 10]

1. **Day of Discovery** (with M. R. DeHaan II)
2. **Hour of Power** (with Robert Schuller)
3. **The Jimmy Swaggart Telecast**
4. **Mother Angelica Live**
5. **The Old Time Gospel Hour** (with Jerry Farwell)
6. **Oral Roberts and You**
7. **PTL Club** (Praise the Lord)
8. **The 700 Club**
9. **Shepherd's Chapel** (with Arnold Murray)
10. **The World Tomorrow**

a. Baton Rouge, Louisiana
b. Birmingham, Alabama
c. Charlotte, North Carolina
d. Garden Grove, California
e. Grand Rapids, Michigan
f. Gravette, Arkansas
g. Lynchburg, Virginia
h. Pasadena, California
i. Tulsa, Oklahoma
j. Virginia Beach, Virginia

Answers: 1. e 2. d 3. a 4. b 5. g 6. i 7. c 8. j 9. f 10. h

TV Dramas in the 1980's

Can you match the following dramas with their locations? [Expert rating: 6 out of 8]

1. **Boone**, starring Tom Byrd, Greg Webb, Barry Corbin

2. **Buck James**, starring Dennis Weaver

3. **Matlock**, starring Andy Griffith

4. **Outlaws**, about four old west cowboys somehow transported to the 1980's

5. **Skag**, starring Karl Malden, Piper Laurie, and Craig Wasson

6. **St. Elsewhere**, starring Ed Flanders, William Daniels, Ed Begley Jr., et. al.

7. **thirty something**, starring Ken Olin and Mel Harris

8. **A Year in the Life**, starring Richard Kiley, Wendy Phillips, Adam Arkin

a. Atlanta, Georgia

b. Boston, Massachusetts

c. Dallas, Texas

d. Houston, Texas

e. Nashville, Tennessee

f. Philadelphia, Pennsylvania

g. Pittsburgh, Pennsylvania

h. Seattle, Washington

Answers: 1. e   2. d   3. a   4. c   5. g   6. b   7. f   8. h

The cast of **thirty something**

© Capital Cities ABC / Shooting Star

Television Shows of the 1980's

1. During the early 1980's the two most popular soap operas were **Dallas** and **Dynasty**. In which cities are these two soap operas located?

2. **Hotel**, based on Arthur Hailey's best-selling novel of the same title, is set in what city?

3. The spy adventure series, **Scarecrow and Mrs. King**, starred Bruce Boxleitner and Kate Jackson. Where was the show set?

4. Before starring in **Spenser: For Hire**, Robert Urich starred in **Vega$** and the adventure series, **Gavilan**. As Robert Gavilan, he played an inventor and a consultant to an oceanography institute. Where was his home located?

5. The **High Mountain Rangers**, starring Robert Conrad and his two sons, is filmed in what local?

6. The comedy, **Hooperman**, stars John Ritter as a detective in what city?

7. Dale Robertson starred as **J. J. Starbuck**, a travelling do-gooder millionaire, in the drama of the same name. What city was his home base?

8. In the 1981 series, **American Dream**, the Novak family (starring Stephen Macht and Karen Carlson) moved from the suburbs to an inner city neighborhood. What were the names of the suburb and the city?

1. Dallas, Texas; Denver, Colorado 2. San Francisco, California 3. Washington, D.C. 4. Malibu, California 5. Lake Tahoe, California 6. San Francisco, California 7. San Antonio, Texas 8. Park Ridge, Illinois; Chicago, Illinois (the show was filmed on location in these cities)

Detective and Police Shows of the 1980's

Can you match the following 1980's police and detective shows with their locals? [Expert rating: 9 out of 12]

1. **Crazy Like a Fox,** starring Jack Warden
2. **Hardcastle & McCormick,** starring Brian Keith and Daniel Hugh Kelly
3. **In the Heat of the Night,** starring Howard Rollins Jr. and Carroll O'Connor
4. **Lady Blue** (short-lived ABC detective series)
5. **Magnum, P.I.,** starring Tom Selleck, John Hillerman, and Roger Mosley
6. **McClain's Law,** starring James Arness and Marshall Colt
7. **Night Heat,** starring Scott Hylands and Allan Royal
8. **Riptide,** starring Perry King, Joe Penny, and Thom Bray
9. **Simon & Simon,** starring Jameson Parker, Gerald McRaney, Tim Reid
10. **Spenser: For Hire,** starring Robert Urich
11. **Whiz Kids,** starring Matthew Laborteaux and Todd Porter
12. **Wise Guy,** starring Ken Wahl and Joan Severance

a. Boston, Massachusetts
b. Calabasas, California
c. Chicago, Illinois
d. Hammond, Louisiana
e. Honolulu, Hawaii
f. Malibu, California
g. Redondo Beach, California
h. San Diego, California
i. San Francisco, California
j. San Pedro, California
k. Toronto, Ontario
l. Vancouver, British Columbia

Answers: 1. i   2. f   3. d   4. c   5. e   6. j   7. k   8. g   9. h   10. a   11. b   12. l

Situation Comedies of the 1980's

Though some comedies are still set in New York or Los Angeles, many 1980's comedies, like 1970's comedies, are spread out all over the country.

1. Can you name two of the four 1980's comedies set in Beverly Hills, California?

2. Name three out of the six 1980's comedies set in Chicago, Illinois.

3. Name three 1980's comedies set in San Francisco, California.

4. Name two 1980's comedies set in Washington, D.C.

5. Name two 1980's comedies set in Boston, Massachusetts.

6. Name two 1980's comedies set in Philadelphia, Pennsylvania.

1. Beverly Hills Buntz; Easy Street; Jennifer Slept Here; The Stockard Channing Show   2. E/R; It Takes Two; Joanie Loves Chachi; Nothing in Common; Punky Brewster; Webster   3. Fitz and Bones; Full House; Good Time Harry; Hooperman; Mr. Merlin; Nobody's Perfect   4. Goodtime Girls; I'm a Big Girl Now; Mr. Smith   5. Cheers; Goodnight, Beantown   6. Amen; Dreams; Pursuit of Happiness

More Comedies of the 1980's

Can you match the following 1980's comedies with their locations? [Expert rating: 10 out of 13]

1. **21 Jump Street**, starring Johnny Depp
2. **Breaking Away**, starring Shaun Cassidy and Barbara Barrie
3. **Channel 99**, new show starring Marilu Henner
4. **Designing Women**, starring Jean Smart, Delta Burke, Annie Potts
5. **Domestic Life**, starring Martin Mull and Christian Brackett-Zika
6. **Double Trouble**, starring Jean Sagal, Liz Sagal, and Donnelly Rhodes
7. **Eisenhower & Lutz** (short-lived 1988 TV pilot)
8. **Ellen Burstyn Show**, starring Ellen Burstyn
9. **Empty Nest**, starring Richard Mulligan, Kristy McNichol, Diane Manoff
10. **Family Ties**, starring Michael J. Fox, Meredith Baxter-Birney
11. **First Impressions** (new 1988 TV pilot)
12. **Frank's Place**, starring Tim Reid
13. **Just the Ten of Us**, starring Bill Kirchenbauer and Deborah Harmon

a. Atlanta, Georgia
b. Baltimore, Maryland
c. Bloomington, Indiana
d. Columbus, Ohio
e. Des Moines, Iowa
f. Elmira, New York
g. Eureka, California
h. Miami, Florida
i. New Orleans, Louisiana
j. Omaha, Nebraska
k. Palm Springs, California
l. Seattle, Washington
m. Vancouver, British Columbia

Answers: 1. m   2. c   3. f   4. a   5. l   6. e   7. k   8. b   9. h   10. d   11. j   12. i   13. g

Even More Comedies of the 1980's

Can you match these 1980's comedies with their locations? [Expert rating: 10 out of 13]

1. **Lewis & Clark**, starring Gabe Kaplan, Guich Koock, and Ilene Graff
2. **Lobo**, starring Claude Akins and Mills Watson
3. **Maggie**, starring Miriam Flynn and James Hampton
4. **Making the Grade**, starring James Naughton and Graham Jarvis
5. **Mama's Family**, starring Vicki Lawrence, Rue McClanahan, Ken Berry
6. **Mr. Belvedere**, starring Bob Uecker and Christopher Hewett
7. **Newhart,** starring Bob Newhart, Mary Frann, and Tom Poston
8. **No Soap, Radio**, starring Steve Guttenberg, Bill Dana, and Fran Ryan
9. **The Popcorn Kid**, about workers in a movie theatre
10. **Private Benjamin**, starring Lorna Patterson and Eileen Brennan
11. **She's the Sheriff**, starring Suzanne Somers
12. **Too Close for Comfort**, starring Ted Knight and Nancy Dussault
13. **Who's the Boss?**, starring Judith Light and Tony Danza

a. Atlanta, Georgia
b. Atlantic City, New Jersey
c. Beaver Falls, Pennsylvania (Pittsburgh)
d. Biloxi, Mississippi
e. Dayton, Ohio
f. Fairfield, Connecticut
g. Kansas City, Missouri
h. Lake Tahoe, California
i. Luckenbach, Texas
j. Norwich, Vermont
k. Raytown, Missouri
l. Saint Louis, Missouri
m. Sausalito, California

Answers: 1. i   2. a   3. e   4. l   5. k   6. c   7. j   8. b   9. g   10. d   11. h   12. m   13. f

New York Locations

Just as in the movies, New York City is often featured as the location for television shows. Do you know the New York City locations of the following television shows?

1. **All in the Family**, 1971-1983 comedy starring Carroll O'Connor and Jean Stapleton

2. **Amos 'n' Andy**, 1951-1953 comedy starring Alvin Chidress and Spencer Williams

3. **Barney Miller**, 1975-1982 comedy starring Hal Linden, Ron Glass, and Abe Vigoda

4. **Car 54, Where Are You?**, 1961-1963 comedy starring Joe E. Ross and Fred Gwynne

5. **Family Affair**, 1966-1971 comedy starring Brian Keith and Sebastian Cabot

6. **The Honeymooners**, 1955-1956 comedy starring Jackie Gleason, Art Carney, Audrey Meadows, and Joyce Randolph

7. **The Jeffersons**, 1975-1984 comedy starring Sherman Hemsley and Isabel Sanford

8. **The Odd Couple**, 1970-1983 comedy starring Tony Randall and Jack Klugman

9. **The Patty Duke Show**, 1963-1966 comedy starring Patty Duke

10. **Welcome Back, Kotter**, 1975-1979 comedy starring Gabe Kaplan and John Travolta

1. 704 Houser Street, Queens 2. Harlem 3. Greenwich Village 4. Bronx 5. 600 East 32nd Street, Manhattan 6. 328 Chauncey Street, Bensonhurst, Brooklyn 7. upper East Side of Manhattan 8. 1049 Park Avenue #1102, Manhattan 9. 8 Remsen Drive, Brooklyn Heights 10. James Buchanan High School, Brooklyn

On Location: Buildings as Stars

Many TV shows, especially in their opening sequences, feature buildings as well as towns and cities. Can you name any of the following buildings? And the city in which they are located?

1. What building was used for the exterior shots of the **Hill Street Blues** station?

2. Where is Angela Channing's (Jane Wyman) **Falcon Crest** mansion actually located?

3. What hotel is used for the exterior shots of the St. Gregory Hotel featured in the soap opera, **Hotel?**

4. What inn is used for the exterior shots of the Stratford Inn, run by Dick Loudon (Bob Newhart) in the comedy, **Newhart?**

5. What is the name of the actual pub used in the exterior shots for the comedy, **Cheers?** And where is it located?

6. What building was used for the exterior shots of the *Daily Planet* building in the **Superman** TV series?

7. Where was the training site for the dolphin who starred in the 1960's drama, **Flipper?**

8. What estate was filmed as the mansion for the 1960's comedy, **The Beverly Hillbillies?** And where was it located?

9. What ranch was used for the location shots of Clayton Farlow's (Howard Keel) ranch in the soap opera, **Dallas**?

10. The main ranch featured in **Dallas** is the Ewing's Southfork Ranch. Where is the actual Southfork Ranch located?

11. What small midwest town was the model for the 1950 soap opera, **Hawkins Falls, Population 6,200**?

12. Where is the new 1988 music variety show, **Rock'n'Roll Palace**, taped?

1. Maxwell Street Precinct in Chicago, Illinois 2. at the Spring Mountain Winery in Saint Helena, California 3. Fairmont Hotel in San Francisco, California 4. the Waybury Inn of East Middlebury, Vermont 5. the Bull & Finch Pub at 84 Beacon Street in Boston, Massachusetts 6. Los Angeles, California City Hall 7. Marathon, Florida 8. the Kirkeby estate in Bel Air area of Los Angeles, California 9. the South Cross Ranch outside of Forney, Texas 10. near Parker, Texas 11. Woodstock, Illinois (population 10,200) 12. Little Darlin's Rock'n'Roll Palace in Kissimmee, Florida

Hometowns of TV characters

Even television characters are born, grow up, and often go on to live somewhere else. Can you name the hometowns of the following TV characters?

1. David Addison (Bruce Willis) in **Moonlighting**
2. Thomas Magnum (Tom Selleck) in **Magnum, P.I.**
3. Anne Kelsey's (Jill Eikenberry) mother in **L.A. Law**
4. Greg (Greg Evigan) and Paul (Paul Shaffer), two singers in the 1977 comedy, **A Year at the Top**
5. Sandy Stockton (Sandy Duncan) in the 1971-1972 comedy, **Funny Face**
6. Ann Marie (Marlo Thomas) in the 1966-1971 comedy, **That Girl**
7. Diana Canova's character in the comedy, **Throb**
8. Sam McCloud (Dennis Weaver) in the 1970-1977 detective show, **McCloud**
9. Charlie Moore (Howard Hesseman) the teacher in the comedy, **Head of the Class**
10. Larry Appleton (Mark Linn-Baker) in the comedy, **Perfect Strangers**
11. Sergeant Jake Rizzo (Lee Majors) in the 1986 detective show, **Sidekicks**
12. Woody (Woody Harrelson), the bartender in **Cheers**
13. Charlene (Jean Smart), one of the **Designing Women**
14. Jack Sierra, one of the pilots in the drama, **Supercarrier**
15. O. S. Willoughby, the electronics whiz on the **Supercarrier**

16. What is the future birthplace of Captain James T. Kirk (William Shatner) of the Starship Enterprise in **Star Trek?**

17. What town claims to be **Superman**'s hometown?

18. Tony Micelli (Tony Danza) of **Who's the Boss?** played for a major league baseball team before becoming a housekeeper. What team did he play for? And what position did he play?

19. What are the hometowns of Sandy Hill and Robb Weller, the hosts of ABC's new infotainment **Home** show?

20. Where is the hometown neighborhood for Fred Roger, the host of the children's show, **Mister Roger's Neighborhood?**

23. In the spring of 1988, Delta Airlines ran an advertisement featuring the soldiers of Company B calling in their plane reservations to return home. What were the hometowns of Company B?

1. Philadelphia, Pennsylvania 2. Detroit, Michigan 3. Waterville, Maine 4. Boise, Idaho 5. Taylorville, Illinois 6. Brewster, New York 7. Buffalo, New York 8. Taos, New Mexico 9. Weiser, Idaho 10. Madison, Wisconsin 11. Cleveland, Ohio 12. Hanover, Indiana 13. Poplar Bluff, Missouri 14. Sheboygan, Wisconsin 15. Salem, Massachusetts 16. Riverside, Iowa 17. Metropolis, Illinois 18. Saint Louis Cardinals (Missouri); second base 19. Centralia, Washington, and Tacoma, Washington 20. 21. Latrobe, Pennsylvania 22.
23. Albuquerque, New Mexico; Atlanta, Georgia; Butte, Montana; Cincinnati, Ohio; Lubbock, Texas; Monroe, Louisiana; New York, New York; Portland, Oregon; San Jose, California

More Hometowns

1. What were the hometowns of the following characters from the hit 1970's comedy series, **M*A*S*H**? Note that Major Margaret "Hot Lips" Houlihan, one of the major characters in the series, did not have a specific hometown because she was an army brat.
   - a. Colonel Sherman Potter (Harry Morgan)
   - b. Captain Benjamin "Hawkeye" Franklin Pierce (Alan Alda)
   - c. Captain "Trapper John" McIntyre (Wayne Rogers)
   - d. Major Frank Burns (Larry Linville)
   - e. Major Charles Emerson Winchester (David Ogden Stiers)
   - f. Corporal Maxwell Klinger (Jamie Farr)
   - g. Corporal Walter "Radar" O'Reilly (Gary Burghoff)

2. What were the hometowns of the following TV talk show hosts?
   - a. Johnny Carson of **The Tonight Show Starring Johnny Carson**
   - b. Phil Donahue of **Donahue**
   - c. Merv Griffin, formerly host of **The Merv Griffin Show**
   - d. David Letterman of **Late Night with David Letterman**
   - e. Oprah Winfrey of **The Oprah Winfrey Show**

1. a. Honolulu, Hawaii (His wife was staying in Honolulu while he was in Korea; he was originally from a small town in Missouri.)
b. Crab Apple Cove, Maine   c. Mill Valley, California   d. Fort Wayne, Indiana   e. Boston, Massachusetts   f. Toledo, Ohio   g. Ottumwa, Iowa
2. a. born in Corning, Iowa; grew up in Norfolk, Nebraska   b. Cleveland, Ohio   c. San Mateo, California   d. Indianapolis, Indiana
e. born in Kosciusko, Mississippi; moved to Milwaukee, Wisconsin at the age of 6; moved to Nashville, Tennessee at the age of 13

The cast of **M*A*S*H**

Towns with Sole Top Billing

In the history of television, only five cities have received sole billing in the naming of a nationwide TV show. Can you name those five cities? To help you out, we have provided some hints below, arranged alphabetically by city name. [Expert rating: 5 out of 5]

1. 1978-? soap opera starring Larry Hagman, Linda Gray, Patrick Duffy, and Victoria Principal
2. 1959-1963 western starring John Smith and Robert Fuller
3. 1965-1967 western starring Neville Brand, Peter Brown, and William Smith
4. 1978-1981 detective drama starring Robert Urich as Dan Tanna
5. 1980's daytime soap opera starring A Martinez and Marcy Walker

1. Dallas, Texas   2. Laramie, Wyoming   3. Laredo, Texas   4. Vega$ (Las Vegas, Nevada)   5. Santa Barbara, California

It could be argued that Cheyenne, Wyoming should also be included because of the popular 1955-1963 western by that name. However, that show took its name not from the city but from the lead character, Cheyenne Bodie, played by Clint Walker.

The cast of **Dallas**

Towns as TV Headliners

As with the movies, towns often get top billing in the naming of a TV show. Can you complete the names of the following shows? If you need help, an alphabetical list of the cities follows this listing. [Expert rating: 19 out of 22]

1. **The _____ Beach Bums**, 1977 comedy starring Christopher Murney and Stuart Pankin
2. **_____ Bill**, 1983-1984 comedy starring Dabney Coleman
3. **_____ Blackie**, 1951-1953 detective starring Kent Taylor, Lois Collier, and Frank Orth
4. **_____ Buntz**, 1987-? detective comedy starring Dennis Franz
5. **_____ City Limits**, 1980's music variety show on public TV
6. **Cutter to _____**, 1983 drama starring Shelley Hack, Jim Metzler, and Alex Baldwin
7. **_____ Days**, 1952-1975 western collection of short stories hosted by Ronald Reagan
8. **_____ International Airport**, 1970-1971 drama starring Lloyd Bridges and Clu Gulager
9. **_____ Knights**, 1986-? detective show starring Michael Beck and Michael Pare
10. **_____ Law**, 1986-? drama starring Harry Hamlin, Jill Eikenberry, Michael Tucker, et.al.
11. **_____ 99**, 1977 police comedy starring Claude Akins, Jerry Reed, and Lucille Benson
12. **_____ Now**, 1980's music talk show starring Ralph Emery
13. **The Pruitts of _____**, 1966-1967 comedy starring Phyllis Diller and Reginald Gardiner
14. **_____ Run**, 1960-1961 adventure starring Keith Larsen, Jeremy Slate, Ron Ely
    (also known as **The Aquanauts**)
15. **_____ Squares**, 1966-? game show with celebrity guests

16. **The Streets of** _____, 1972-1977 detective show starring Karl Malden and Michael Douglas
17. **The** _____ **Teddy Bears**, 1971 short-lived comedy starring Dean Jones, Art Metrano, Jamie Farr
18. _____ **Territory**, 1957-1959 western starring Pat Conway and Richard Eastham
19. _____ **Town**, 1959-1960 western starring Joel McCrea, Jody McCrea, and Carlos Romero
20. _____ **U**, 1967 summer musical show hosted by Rick Nelson
21. _____ **Vice**, 1985-? detective show starring Don Johnson and Philip Michael Thomas
22. _____ **Hillbillies**, 1962-1971 hit comedy starring Buddy Epson, Irene Ryan, Donna Douglas

Here are the town names that complete the names of the shows: Austin, Beverly Hills (twice), Boston, Buffalo, Chicago, Death Valley, Hollywood, Houston (twice), Los Angeles, Malibu (twice), Miami, Nashville (twice), San Francisco (twice), San Pedro, Southampton, Tombstone, Wichita

1. San Pedro, California 2. Buffalo, New York 3. Boston, Massachusetts 4. Beverly Hills, California 5. Austin, Texas 6. Houston, Texas 7. Death Valley, California 8. San Francisco, California 9. Houston, Texas 10. (LA) Los Angeles, California 11. Nashville, Tennessee 12. Nashville, Tennessee 13. Southampton, New York 14. Malibu, California 15. Hollywood, California 16. San Francisco, California 17. Chicago, Illinois 18. Tombstone, Arizona 19. Wichita, Kansas 20. Malibu, California 21. Miami, Florida 22. Beverly Hills, California

Fictional TV Towns of the 1950's

Many television shows are set in fictional communities. Can you name the fictional towns of the following 1950's shows? [Expert rating: 7 out of 9]

1. **The Aldrich Family**, comedy starring House Jameson and Leona Powers
2. **Dennis the Menace**, comedy starring Jay North and Herbert Anderson
3. **The Deputy**, western starring Henry Fonda, Allan Case, Wallace Ford
4. **The Howdy Dowdy Show**, children's show starring Buffalo Bob, Howdy Doody, and Clarabell the Clown
5. **Johnny Ringo**, western starring Don Durant and Karen Sharpe
6. **Leave It to Beaver**, comedy starring Jerry Mathers and Barbara Billingsley
7. **Phil Silvers Show**, comedy starring Phil Silvers, Harvey Lembeck, Paul Ford
8. **The Rifleman**, western starring Chuck Connors, John Crawford, Paul Fix
9. **Superman**, adventure starring George Reeves, Noel Neill, Jack Larson

a. Centerville, USA
b. Doodyville, USA
c. Hillsdale
d. Mayfield

e. Metropolis
f. North Fork, New Mexico
g. Roseville (Fort Baxter), Kansas
h. Silver City, Arizona
i. Velardi, Arizona

Answers: 1. a   2. c   3. h   4. b   5. i   6. d   7. g   8. f   9. e

Fictional TV Towns of the 1960's

The 1960's also featured many fictional towns. Can you match the following shows with the fictional towns in which they were set? [Expert rating: 6 out of 9]

1. **The Andy Griffith Show**, comedy starring Andy Griffith, Don Knotts
2. **Bus Stop**, drama starring Marilyn Maxwell and Rhodes Reason
3. **Empire**, western starring Richard Egan, Terry Moore, Ryan O'Neal
4. **Hazel**, comedy starring Shirley Booth
5. **It's a Man's World**, comedy starring Glenn Corbett and Ted Bessell
6. **The Long Hot Summer**, soap opera starring Edmond O'Brien
7. **The Munsters**, comedy starring Fred Gwynne, Yvonne DeCarlo, Al Lewis
8. **My Three Sons**, comedy starring Fred MacMurray and William Demarest
9. **Pistol's 'n' Petticoats**, western starring Ann Sheridan and Douglas Fowley

a. Bryant Park
b. Cordella, Ohio
c. Frenchman's Bend
d. Hydsberg, New York
e. Mayberry, North Carolina
f. Mesa, New Mexico
g. Mockingbird Heights
h. Sunrise, Colorado
i. Wretched, Colorado

Answers: 1. e   2. h   3. f   4. d   5. b   6. c   7. g   8. a   9. i

Fictional TV Towns of the 1970's

Can you name the fictional towns of the following 1970's shows? [Expert rating: 7 out of 11]

1. **America 2-Night**, satire starring Martin Mull and Fred Willard
2. **Dan August**, detective show starring Burt Reynolds and Norman Fell
3. **Doc Elliot**, drama starring James Franciscus, Noah Beery, Bo Hopkins
4. **Hec Ramsey**, western starring Richard Boone, Richard Lenz, Harry Morgan
5. **The Kallikaks**, comedy starring David Huddleston and Edie McClurg
6. **Mary Hartman, Mary Hartman**, soap opera starring Louise Lasser
7. **Mulligan's Stew**, comedy starring Lawrence Pressman and Elinor Donahue
8. **The New Andy Griffith Show**, comedy starring Andy Griffith
9. **The Paul Lynde Show**, comedy starring Paul Lynde and Elizabeth Allen
10. **Sara**, western starring Brenda Vaccaro
11. **The Waverly Wonders**, comedy starring Joe Namath

a. Alta Coma, California
b. Birchfield, California
c. Eastfield, Wisconsin
d. Fernwood, Ohio
e. Gideon, Colorado
f. Greenwood
g. Independence, Colorado
h. New Prospect, Oklahoma
i. Nowhere, California
j. Ocean Grove, California
k. Santa Luisa, California

Answers: 1. a   2. k   3. e   4. h   5. i   6. d   7. b   8. f   9. j   10. g   11. c

More Fictional TV Towns of the 1970's

1. In the 1974 drama, **Apple's Way**, George Apple (Ronny Cox) takes his family away from the rat race of Los Angeles to return to his hometown? What was the name of his fictional hometown?

2. Glenn Ford starred as Sheriff Sam Cade in the 1971 drama, **Cade's County**. What was the name of the county and the county seat of which he was sheriff? In what state was the county located?

3. **Carter Country,** the 1977-1979 comedy starring Victor French and Kene Holliday, was set in a small town just down the road from Plains, Georgia (hometown of President Jimmy Carter). What was the name of the fictional town?

4. **The New Land** was a short-lived adventure series (starring Bonnie Bedelia, Scott Thomas, and Kurt Russell) about the hardships of Swedish imigrants in 1858 America. In what small town was the story set? Where was the series filmed?

5. Name the following four series whose titles are also the names of towns in which they were set:

   a. _____, historical miniseries starring Robert Conrad, Richard Chamberlain, and many others.

   b. _____ **2-Night,** a satire of TV talk shows, starring Martin Mull and Fred Willard.

   c. _____, fall 1976 drama starring John Savage and Gig Young (based on John O'Hara novel).

   d. _____, a 1971 western starring James Garner and Stuart Margolin (set in 1914).

1. Appleton, Iowa 2. Madrid County; Madrid, California 3. Clinton Corner's, Georgia 4. Solna, Minnesota; on location in Oregon and California
5. a. Centennial (Colorado) b. Fernwood (Ohio) c. Gibbsville (Pennsylvania) d. Nichols (Arizona)

Fictional TV Towns of the 1980's

1. In 1981, after a successful run as Jim Rockford on **The Rockford Files,** James Garner returned to star in another western set in a small town in Arizona. In this series he played Bret Maverick, a character he had played some 20 years earlier in the hit western, **Maverick.** This new series, titled **Bret Maverick,** however, did not last very long. With that introduction, can you name the location for this new series?

2. After **M.A.S.H.** went off the air, three of its stars (Harry Morgan, Jamie Farr, and William Christopher) were reunited in a comedy series, **Aftermash,** about the goings-on at a veteran's hospital. Where was this hospital located?

3. **Flamingo Road** (starring Howard Duff, Morgan Fairchild, and Mark Harmon) was another soap opera that tried, unsuccessfully, to imitate the success of **Dallas.** In what fictitious southern town was it set?

4. The 1980 comedy **Flo** was a spinoff of the hit comedy, **Alice,** in which Polly Holliday stars as Flo Castleberry, who retires her waitress shoes to open a roadhouse in her hometown. What was the name of her hometown?

5. Four years after leaving the hit series, **All in the Family,** Sally Struthers returned to star as Gloria Bunker Stivic in a new comedy series, **Gloria.** In this series, she plays an assistant to Dr. Willard Adams (Burgess Meredith), a veternarian in upstate New York. What was the name of the small town where she now lived?

6. **Gun Shy** was a very short-lived comedy western takeoff of the Walt Disney movie comedies, **The Apple Dumpling Gang** and **The Apple Dumpling Gang Strikes Again** (starring Bill Bixby, Don Knotts, and Tim Conway). In what small California town was the TV series (starring Barry Van Dyke, Tim Thomerson, and Geoffrey Lewis) set?

7. **Murder, She Wrote**, the hit mystery series starring Angela Lansbury, is set in what fictitious New England village?

8. Jerry Orbach and Barbara Babcock star in the detective series, **The Law and Harry McGraw**, a spinoff from **Murder, She Wrote**. In what real New England city is the show set?

9. Can you complete the titles of the following two series with the names of the fictitious towns that are part of the titles?

   a. **The _____ Blues**, 1983 soap opera (from the creators of **Hill Street Blues** and starring Kelly Harmon, Michael Nouri, and Dennis Franz) told the story of a minor-league baseball team.

   b. **When in _____** is a new comedy series starring Kate Capshaw as a New Yorker who moves to a small town in North Dakota and has to adjust to the new way of life.

1. Sweetwater, Arizona 2. River Bend, Missouri 3. Truro, Florida 4. Cowtown, Texas 5. Foxridge, New York 6. Quake City, California 7. Cabot Cove, Maine 8. Boston, Massachusetts 9. a. Bay City (California) b. Rome (North Dakota)

Index of Movies

127

130

Index to Television Shows

H

Hagen, 83
Happy, 92
Happy Days, 7, 96
Harbor Command, 83
Hardcastle & McCormick, 83, 105
Harrigan & Son, 83
Harry-O, 83, 90
Hart to Hart, 83, 93
Have Gun, Will Travel, 86
Hawaii Five-O, 83, 93
Hawaiian Eye, 83, 84
Hawaiian Heat, 83
Hawk, 83
Hawkins Falls, Population 6,200, 111
Hayloft Hoedown, 81
Hazel, 121
Head of the Class, 112
Hec Ramsey, 122
Hee Haw Honeys, 98
Hello, Larry, 98
Hennesey, 80
Here Comes the Brides, 92
High Chaparral, 86
High Mountain Rangers, 104
Hill Street Blues, 110, 125
Hollywood Squares, 118
The Home Show, 113
Honey West, 83
The Honeymooners, 109
Hooperman, 83, 104, 106
Hotel, 104, 110
Hotel de Paree, 85
Hour of Power, 101
House Calls, 96

Houston Knights, 118
The Howdy Dowdy Show, 120
Hunter, 83

I

I Cover Times Square, 83
I Dream of Jeannie, 92
I Love Lucy, 90
I'm a Big Girl Now, 106
I'm the Law, 83
In the Heat of the Night, 105
The Innocent and the Damned, 100
The Investigator, 83
The Investigators, 83
Ironside, 83
It Takes Two, 106
It's a Man's World, 121

J

J J Starbuck, 104
Jake and the Fatman, 83
James at 15, 100
The Jeffersons, 109
Jennifer Slept Here, 106
Jessie, 83
Jimmy Hughes, Rookie Cop, 83
The Jimmy Swaggart Telecast, 101
Joanie Loves Chachi, 106
Joe and Sons, 98
Joe's World, 98
Johnny Midnight, 83
Johnny Ringo, 120
Johnny Staccato, 83
Judd, For the Defense, 84
Just the Two of Us, 107
Justice, 83

K

The Kallikaks, 122
Karen, 96
Kate Loves a Mystery, 83
Kate McShane, 83
Khan!, 83
Kingston: Confidential, 83
Klondike, 86
Knight Rider, 83
Kojak, 83
Kolchak: The Night Stalker, 93

L

LA Law, 112, 118
Lady Blue, 83, 105
Laramie, 116
Laredo, 116
Late Night with David Letterman, 114
Laverne & Shirley, 96
The Law and Harry McGraw, 83, 125
Law of the Plainsman, 85
The Lawless Years, 83
Leave It to Beaver, 120
The Legend of Jesse James, 86
Lewis & Clark, 108
The Lieutenant, 88
The Life and Legend of Wyatt Earp, 90
Little House on the Prairie, 100
Lobo, 108
The Long Hot Summer, 121
Longstreet, 93
Lou Grant, 100
Love on a Rooftop, 92
Lucas Tanner, 100
The Lucy Show, 90
Lum & Abner Show, 80

Index of States and Cities

Jackson, 41
Kosciusko, 114
Natchez, 48, 59
Oxford, 54

Missouri
Bland, 8
Boring, 8
Fulton, 21
Hannibal, 29
Jefferson City, 80
Kansas City, 35, 58, 61, 65, 81, 98, 108
Poplar Bluff, 112-113
Raytown, 108
Saint Joseph, 47, 86
Saint Louis, 15, 45, 58, 59, 66, 91, 108, 113
Springfield, 81
Webster Groves, 100

Montana
Billings, 78
Butte, 38, 113

Nebraska
Boys Town, 20
Fremont, 54
Omaha, 20, 78, 107
Norfolk, 114
Sandwich, 9
Tecumseh, 50-51
Valentine, 8

Nevada
Bonanza, 8
Boulder City, 44-45

Carson City, 30
Las Vegas, 20, 19, 29, 38, 44-45, 46, 56, 59, 60, 61, 91, 96, 116
Reno, 59, 66
Virginia City, 67, 86

New Hampshire
Hanover, 17
Portsmouth, 44-45, 72

New Jersey
Atlantic City, 19, 64, 93, 108
Camden, 13
Dover, 48-49
Fort Lee, 13
Hackensack, 42-43, 49
Hoboken, 98
Lakehurst, 49
Newark, 38, 93
Passaic, 13
Paterson, 39
Princeton, 17
Secaucus, 49, 61-63
Tenafly, 48
Weehawken, 15
West Orange, 13

New Mexico
Albuquerque, 46, 64, 72, 93, 100, 113
Jal, 8
Santa Fe, 17, 37, 39, 55, 58, 67, 73, 85
Taos, 112-113
Texico, 9
Truchas, 55
Truth or Consequences, 77

New York
Albany, 36
Amityville, 61
Brewster, 112-113
Brooklyn, 14-15, 56, 109
Buffalo, 118-119
Elmira, 107
Endwell, 128
Great Neck, 98
Ithaca, 36
Lake Placid, 37
New Rochelle, 80, 92
New York, 14-15, 18, 32, 35, 38, 39, 44-45, 46, 52, 56, 57, 58, 61-63, 82-83, 90-91, 113, 109, 125
Niagara Falls, 66
North Pole, 8
Nyack, 54
Pearl River, 80
Peekskill, 98
Pelham, 80
Poughkeepsie, 27
Riverdale, 79
Saratoga Springs, 44-45, 67
Schenectady, 77
Southampton, 118-119
Tuckahoe, 98
West Point, 21, 57, 73
Woodstock, 14-15, 67

North Carolina
Asheville, 50-51
Charlotte, 101
Matrimony, 9
Old Trap, 9

Help Wanted

In the fall of 1989, Ad-Lib Publications is planning to publish three more books in this series about towns and cities in the United States and Canada. The three books are as follows:

Music Cities, U.S.A. — This book will focus on towns and cities which have been featured in songs of all sorts, from rock'n'roll to country music, from *Chattanooga Choo Choo* to *Wichita Lineman*. Over 400 cities and songs will be featured!

Celebration Cities, U.S.A. — This book will feature towns and cities which sponsor various fun competitions, from the World Freefall Convention to various oddball world championship events (worm races, motorized bar stoll races, frog eating contests, and many more delights). Also Halls of Fame, Bowl Games, World Capitals (such as the mule and placemat capitals of the world), and more.

Trivial Towns: From Start (Louisiana) to Endwell (New York) — This book will feature all sorts of odd, wonderful, delightful, funny, and outrageous town names (much like those listed in the introduction to this book). Over 2000 towns will be featured. When known, I'll also indicate how they got their names.

Anyway, I need your help if these books are going to be the best they can be. So, please send me the names, songs, events, and stories about towns you know. If you send me something I don't already have, I'll send you an autographed copy of the book when it is published (and list your name in the preface to the book). Thanks for your help. Send information to:

John Kremer, c/o Ad-Lib Publications, 51 N. Fifth Street, Fairfield, IA 52556-3226